*Making
Twig
Garden
Furniture*

Also by Abby Ruoff

Making Twig Furniture & Household Things
Weddings With More Love Than Money

Making Twig Garden Furniture

ABBY RUOFF

Photographs by
ABBY RUOFF

Illustrations by
SIA KASKAMANIDIS

Hartley & Marks
PUBLISHERS

Published by

HARTLEY & MARKS PUBLISHERS INC.

P. O. Box 147   3661 West Broadway
Point Roberts, WA   Vancouver, BC
98281   V6R 2B8

LIBRARY OF CONGRESS CATALOGING-IN-PUBLICATION DATA
Ruoff, Abby.
    Making twig garden furniture / Abby Ruoff.
      p.   cm.
    ISBN 0-88179-144-X
    1. Outdoor furniture. 2. Furniture making. 3. Twigs. I. Title.
TT197.5.09R86   1997
684..1'8—dc21   96-52936
                                                  CIP

Design and composition by The Typeworks
Cover design by The Typeworks
Set in WALBAUM, SCALA SANS, & GOUDY SANS

Printed in the U.S.A.

TO BENJAMIN AND SAMUEL

"Children are like flowers in a garden;
tend to them and nurture them, and
they will grow strong and beautiful."
— MY GRANDMOTHER

Acknowledgments

I want to express my appreciation to Sue Tauber for planting the first seeds, and to Vic Marks, for his faith in this project. I wish also to thank Susan Juby, my editor, who told me from the beginning that she was "familiar with my work," and waited patiently until every last word was written, and to Annalisa Taylor, Hartley & Marks' promotions coordinator, who has faith in my ability to articulate.

I would like to thank my neighbors who invited me into their gardens: Kristine Flones of Whittenberg, Leza of Woodstock, Gerry Jacobs of Easton Lane, and Malcolm Rose of Bearsville.

To Carl, my husband, who taught me the language of the forest and encouraged me to write this book, I am forever grateful.

Contents

Grandfather's Planting Twigs

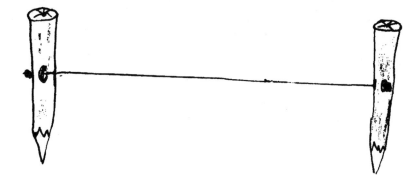

A homemade gardening aid,
remarkable in its simplicity and usefulness.

Whittle the ends of two 12″ long, 3/4″ diameter twigs;
drill a hole through each twig 3″ down from the top;
thread six yards of strong twine through both holes,
and knot the ends.

Use like a compass to lay out circles and arcs,
or measure and divide straight lines.

Introduction

The Cedar Gate   Tannersville, N. Y.

THEY ARE SIMPLE THINGS. A TRELLIS. A BIRDFEEDER.
A chair. But look again, and these simple pieces are practical and
ingenious: green willow shoots are shaped into arches to support
climbing vines; a hollow white birch log holds a supply of bird
seed; and a few forked branches are nailed together to form a
chair. Twig furniture and gardens are natural partners, throw-
backs to a simpler time, and all the things we love: a rose-covered
arbor, a fence of woven willow shoots to border and divide the
salad greens, a scarecrow formed of sticks and twigs to guard the
corn, a mixture of country memories and lazy summer afternoons. Of the wide range of garden and outdoor furnishings
available today, made of everything from cast iron to stone, nothing seems better suited to the garden than pieces fashioned from
branches, bark, and vines. The simple charm of a natural seat
tucked in the garden reflects the best of a rustic tradition; here
the beauty of field, forest, and garden embrace.

In the late 1800s the creation of grand and glorious gardens
became a colorful way of displaying prosperity, and the wealthy
became preoccupied with garden ornament. The Victorian era,

and its romanticized vision of nature, created the perfect setting for rustic work, and landscape designers began to place seats of twisted, gnarled rhododendron and laurel in unexpected corners and along curving paths. Soon the Golden Age of rustic garden furnishings gave way to the more practical side of the gardener's nature, and simple bean poles, tomato supports, rose trellises, and arbors were fashioned out of available twigs. Today increased environmental awareness finds more people moving their lifestyles out of doors. Not only are they eating and entertaining on the porch or in the garden, but very often they are growing their own pesticide-free produce. As garden activity grows, so too does the popularity of garden furnishings. Soon after the publication of my first rustic twig book, *Making Twig Furniture*, 1991, many readers wrote requesting plans for rustic designs to be used in the garden, such as trellis work, arbors, and fanciful birdhouses and feeders. This book is a direct result of those requests.

Designing these rustic furnishings has rekindled happy childhood memories of gardens where twigs were used to stake giant sunflowers, and helped to support vined beans and peas. I remember with fondness attaching short branches to empty seed packages to mark the tidy rows in my grandfather's vegetable garden. Every year, as sure as spring turns to summer, my grandmother's flower garden rose up under the ancient lilacs. The same twig bench remained tucked into a clearing between the day lilies and the phlox in all seasons. That bench, wobbly though it was, served as a special place for childhood dreams. I think it was here that I first saw the connection between the tree and the furniture. The bench had remained in the same spot for so many years that it seemed to grow right out of the ground. The magic of its creation fascinated me, and rustic furniture became part of my earliest memories.

Gardeners and craftspeople share a common bond. The creative challenges are the same whether you are laying out plants in a landscape, or designing a chair. There is something very fulfilling about working with your hands. The personal expression that helps to make a garden great is part of the same creative energy that builds rustic twig furnishings. Various demands on my time have forced me to neglect my own gardens for several years, but now as a result of these new projects I have expanded my herb garden and flower beds. In truth, I cannot tell if the garden is a backdrop for the furniture, or the furniture is the reason for the garden. Sometimes in my dreams, waking or sleeping, I think I have recaptured the details of that crudely nailed together bench in grandmother's garden where I spent so many happy summer hours.

Outdoor furnishings, like their indoor counterparts, require a sense of belonging or purpose. It is important to consider dimensions and scale when placing outdoor furnishings, for it is the total arrangement that creates the beautiful garden. Center a pedestal sundial in a herb garden, hang a windowbox on a kitchen garden fence, or position trelliage along a brick city wall or weathered barn for a distinctive display. A few well-chosen rustic garden twig elements will help turn any outdoor area into a cozy retreat, and learning to make twig garden furnishings is easier than you think.

Remember, interesting and appealing areas are created when ingenuity and resourcefulness take precedence. Use this book as a guide—fine tune your creativity and educate your eyes to make something wonderful out of twigs and branches.

There are projects here for every skill level; beginner, intermediate, or experienced, and they are varied enough to interest and challenge any craftsperson.

Note that the pattern pieces need to be enlarged on a photocopier, and that several pieces need to be enlarged by more than 200%, which is the beyond the capacity of most copiers, so they will need to be enlarged twice.

Your local copy shop should be able to do your enlargements if you don't have access to a machine.

CHAPTER 1

Finding
the
Wood

RUSTIC GARDEN FURNITURE DESIGNS ARE DICTATED
by the character of the wood they are made from, so it is important to be able to identify various trees and shrubs and to famil-
iarize yourself with their individual characteristics. Since not all
trees are available in all regions or climates, I encourage you to
experiment with your local materials. You will also want to learn
various cultivating techniques to avoid destroying existing
stands so they are preserved for future generations.

For the purposes of this book, you should know that trees are
single-stemmed plants that attain a height of at least 15 feet,
while shrubs are often multi-stemmed and generally grow to
about 10 feet. Twigs are young limbs, called shoots when they are

new growth, and are usually not more than two inches in diameter. Learning to recognize species under various growing conditions is not always easy. Many trees that grow at high elevations on mountains are twisted and sprawling as a result of a short growing season and strong winds, but at low levels they stand tall and straight. When searching for wood, you should carry a tree identification manual to help you recognize trees by their leaves, flowers, fruits, and bark.

A very good manual for tree identification is the series by the Nature Study Guild, Box 972, Berkeley, Calif., 94701. Send for their catalog for your area, such as *Pacific Coast Tree Finder*, *Rocky Mountain Tree Finder*, *Desert Tree Finder*, or *Winter Tree Finder*. These are small manuals that can be kept in your pocket or in the glove compartment of your car. Other helpful manuals are *The Simon and Schuster Pocket Guide to Trees*, *Trees and Shrubs (Northeastern and Central North America)*, and *The Peterson Field Guide Series*.

COLLECTING TWIGS AND BRANCHES

If you do not own your own "back 40" country acres where you can gather twigs and limbs, here are some lessons in creative harvesting. One woman who lives in a small city told me she befriended the park workers in the city park. As they prune trees, they save some of the longer branches for her. She rewards them at holidays with homemade pies, and now has several twig chairs and baskets in her apartment. I do not want to tell you to wish for a calamity, but a friend of mine in Iowa recently experienced a dreadful ice storm, with tree branches breaking off under the weight of the ice. While his neighbors were bemoaning the loss of favorite trees, he was busy gathering twigs for future projects. Be alert for innovative ways to secure your materials. Fruit orchards, such as apple, pear, or cherry, can be another good source of materials. Search out sites where developers and builders are working in your area. All too often such commercial ventures will destroy precious natural resources. Although this is heartbreaking, you can put the cut trees to good use, rather than seeing them wasted in a burning pit. I have even heard about someone who approached a builder to obtain some cut trees, and was offered pay to cart them away. Now there is an agreeable situation! Friendly farmers or loggers might be glad to sell you a small amount of twigs and limbs for a nominal charge. There are many innovative ways to obtain materials, and if you are enterprising I know you will succeed.

How to Choose and Gather Twigs

Always select fresh materials. Cut the twigs with care and be sure you don't pull the roots out. If you are collecting thin branches, such as willow, leave more than you remove, so that you preserve the plant and are assured a plentiful future supply. Use only sharp cutting tools (axes, saws, or clippers), and never rip or tear the branches, as this can destroy a living plant. Examine the twigs for insects or larvae, and try to avoid any pests. If these seem to be a problem, treat the wood with a safe garden insecticide before building your furniture.

How to Examine the Twigs for Larvae

When you are gathering twigs and poles, take time to check for insect activity, since you will not want to build furniture out of infested wood. Wood-eating insects on living trees are relatively rare. Most wood eaters feed on dead trees. If your cut wood supply is kept outside for a prolonged period, it will become a target for bugs. Examine the branches for tiny holes or deep channels. This is not necessarily a sure-fire method for detecting live insects, but it is a clue for further investigation. If you suspect that a branch is infested, separate it from the rest of your supply for a week, and check it daily. If you find small piles of sawdust around or near the holes, the limb should be discarded.

Watch for twig-boring insects when you are harvesting thin twigs and vines. The larvae of beetles often bore through tender twigs and small branches, killing large portions of a tree's crown. When you are out collecting twigs, remember to look up. Learn to recognize the signs of tree damage.

If you find signs of insect activity after your piece is built, you will have to spray it with an insecticide. Several safe, effective insecticides are available today, and more are being developed. Check with your local nursery or hardware store, and make sure the product you choose is safe for indoor and outdoor use. You should use a product that is made with a natural *botanical pyrethrin* base, for pieces that will be used outside. Be sure to read the label carefully. It is always best to apply the insecticide outdoors.

ALDER   Eight species of native alder grow rapidly in North America, often forming thickets in moist soil. All alder trees have irregularly toothed, prominently veined, oval or oblong leaves. The red alder tree of the Pacific Northwest often reaches heights of 30 to 40 feet, and the outside edges of its leaves are rolled under. The white alder, although usually smaller, is similar to the red alder, except that its leaves are flat. The Sitka alder is distinctive because of its smooth grey-green bark, covered with warty clusters. The undersides of its outermost leaves are glossy and sticky. The thin leaf alder and the mountain alder have oblong leaves, two to three inches wide, with orange-brown midribs that sport rusty brown hairs. The undersides of its leaves are dull, not sticky. The Arizona alder, which grows in the southwestern United States, has slightly smaller leaves with a yellow midrib and a smooth, grey to brownish bark. The seaside alder, on the other hand, grows on the east coast. With its round-topped crown of zigzag branches, it is quite easy to identify.

The alder is a relatively obscure tree, and it is often overlooked as a viable wood for twig furnishings. However, as a close cousin to birch and hazelnut, its pliable branches are invaluable. Alder can be used to make trellises and fences, and to form the backs on garden chairs. Larger pieces can be used for the garden gate.

Where Alder Trees Grow

Most alder grows in the western regions of the United States and Canada. It is easily distinguishable in the spring, when staminate catkins cast a distinctive greenish-brown hue over the surrounding area. Alder is found around lakes, along streams and creek beds, and in open swamps.

BEECH There are almost 100 species of beech native to North America. They are handsome, deciduous trees with short-stemmed, prominently veined, elliptical leaves, three to six inches long. Their smooth bark is blue-grey and commonly blotched with dark grey speckling and thin split lines. On older beech trees a smoky, dark tone is often noticeable on one side of the trunk, with still darker areas around the base. Young beech trees are easily recognizable by their deep red-brown buds, covered with cream-colored flecks.

Beech wood is tight-grained, heavy, and strong. Because the bark on beech trees is strong and tight, it does not peel off easily, making it particularly desirable for making twig chairs and plant stands.

Where Beech Trees Grow
Beech trees are usually found in deep forests, surrounded by oaks or maples. They grow from southern Ontario to Nova Scotia, from central Wisconsin to Maine, and south to Texas and northern Florida.

BIRCH While you'll find information on white paper birch in the "Working with Bark and Vine" chapter, there are many other useful birches growing throughout most of North America. One of them is the low-growing Alaskan shrub called ground birch, which is an important summer food for northern animals. Yellow birch yields bark that is yellowish to bronze, which peels into thin, narrow strips. Water birch is a small, slender tree, often with drooping branches and a dark brown bark. River birch has a scaly, grey-black trunk on older trees, and thin, pinkish bark on young trees. The river birch's trunk is often divided into multi-arched limbs, while the blueleaf birch grows most commonly as a shrub, with a rosy-hued bark that does not peel. Yukon birch is a stately tree that often reaches heights of 25 feet. It can be identified by its dark brown bark and white lenticel clusters (ventilating pores in the bark). Black birch is set apart from the other birches with its mahogany-red bark, smooth and glossy in young trees, and rough and scaly in older trees. Its leaves and bark have a sweet, minty aroma, and it is sometimes called sweet birch. Birch leaves vary in shape, but all have prominent veins and short leaf stems.

The strength of birch and the coloring of its bark make it very desirable for furniture. Its sturdy limbs are useful for shelves, planters, bird houses, and feeders.

Where Birch Trees Grow

Birch trees grow rapidly, often forming extensive forests in the north. Yellow and black birch grow along the east coast, from northern Canada into the United States as far south as Georgia. Water birch and Yukon birch grow in the western United States and Canada. River birch is the only native birch that grows at low elevations, along streams in the southeastern United States. Blueleaf birch is found in Maine and eastern Quebec, along the St. Lawrence River valley. Its blue-green leaves make it easy to identify.

BOX ELDER   The box elder has three-leaflet leaves with jagged edges, similar to maple leaves Its bark is pastel red, purple, or bright green, often coated with a thin white haze. Box elder branches are brittle when dry, so it may be helpful to soak them in a bucket of water until ready for use. These colorful and glossy twigs are suitable for small projects such as the hanging herb and flower drying rack.

Where Box Elder Trees Grow

Box elder grows in the western United States, from Illinois to Colorado and northern Texas up to the Pacific Northwest. It is an extremely adaptable tree, growing on high or low ground, in sunlight or shade, in moist or dry areas.

CEDAR Most cedar wood is aromatic, including some cypress and juniper. Cedar foliage is compact and dark with a slightly prickly texture. Incense cedars are covered with dark brown, deeply furrowed bark. Northern white cedar and Atlantic white cedar also have deeply furrowed barks, ranging in color from ash-grey to reddish-brown. Western red cedar is distinguishable by its vertically ridged, brownish-grey, shredded bark. Port Orford cedar has dark green foliage similar to the Western red cedar's, but the scales on its branches are tighter. Alaska cedar is a smaller tree with yellow-green foliage and a rougher texture than the Port Orford. It usually has grey shaggy bark and thin scales. Its interior wood is most often yellow in appearance.

Sturdy cedar limbs were used for the vine trimmed garden bench. Their shaggy bark adds texture and interest to any project. Cedar poles are especially useful where strong supports are required, such as the summer house.

Where Cedar Trees Grow

Cedar in one form or another is plentiful throughout most of the United States and Canada. It is found alongside water bodies from North Dakota to Maine and southern Ontario, and then south to central Texas and northern Florida. In the northwest, throughout Oregon, Washington, and British Columbia, cedars of various types grow in abundance. Its shaggy bark, remarkable shape, and unique aroma make it easy to locate.

CHERRY Cherry trees grow in abundance throughout most parts of the northern hemisphere, often in cool regions. Black cherry is usually easy to identify because of its distinctive color. In the sapling stage, its bark is smooth and reddish-brown, turning dark grey and flaky on mature trees. All cherry trees have simple, alternating leaves that are two to five inches long, a bit leathery, and serrated along their edges.

The strength and beautiful coloring of the young cherry saplings make them ideal for twig chair parts. The wood is usually free from warping, but should be well-seasoned before it is used because it shrinks during seasoning.

Where Cherry Trees Grow

Cherry trees of one type or another are common throughout most of North America. The black cherry grows in rich soils and woods from southeastern Manitoba to Nova Scotia, and from eastern South Dakota to Maine and south to eastern Texas and central Florida.

The pin cherry grows 15 to 25 feet tall, and is found across most of Canada to Nova Scotia, and as far south as South Carolina to the east and Utah in the west.

The common chokecherry is a shrub or small tree found in most of North America, except in the extreme southern areas of Texas, Arkansas, Louisiana, Alabama, Georgia, and Florida. It can grow 25 feet tall and up to eight inches in diameter. The chokecherry has white flowers in the spring, and tiny, dark red cherries in the summer, usually about one-third of an inch in diameter.

The bitter cherry has red to black cherries, about half an inch in diameter. Distinguishable by its brownish bark with horizontal, orange lenticels, it can grow to 40 feet and 18 inches in diameter. The bitter cherry occurs along the western half of North America—from British Columbia and Alberta throughout most of Washington and Oregon—and as far east and south as parts of Nevada and Arizona.

Hollyleaf cherry has egg-shaped, evergreen leaves, one to two inches long and an inch wide. Along with the rare Catalina cherry, it grows along the extreme western coast of California.

BALD CYPRESS The bald cypress, also known as southern or red cypress, can grow to grand heights of 100 feet. It has yellow-green needles that turn brown before falling in the autumn. Bald cypress also produces wrinkled cones about an inch wide that mature in one season. Its branches are often draped with Spanish moss.

Bald cypress forms "knees," which are really branches that grow out of its widespread underground root system. These sharp, pointed extensions project above the surface. Craftspeople often use these "knees" to create lamp bases and sculptures.

Bald cypress is most often used to build chairs, loveseats, and planters. Its naturally pale bark is beautiful left in its natural state, and looks lovely indoors or on covered porches. Cypress will weather to a soft grey. Left outside for a season, your weathered cypress piece will be appreciated for its subtle coloring.

Where Cypress Trees Grow

The bald cypress is probably familiar to those who live along the southern part of the United States. It grows in large forests, especially in the wet coastal plains of Florida. Although not all bald cypress grows in water, it is abundant where periodic flooding is common. Most often associated with rustic work from Florida, the species has a large growing area, ranging from southern New Jersey to Florida, along the Atlantic Coastal Plain, across the Gulf Coast Lowlands into Texas and Mexico, and up the Mississippi basin as far as Illinois and Indiana.

EUCALYPTUS (BLUE GUM)

Eucalyptus bark is usually thin and reddish-brown in color. It peels off in long strips, revealing a creamy-white or grey underbark. Its leathery curved leaves are pale green, six to 12 inches long, with a sharp tip. The blue gum can grow to heights of 200 feet.

Eucalyptus benefits from frequent pruning, and 10-year-old trees can provide a continuous supply of branches useful for chair parts, and a variety of other twig projects.

Where Eucalyptus Trees Grow

The branches and bark of over 200 species of Australian eucalyptus trees are widely used in constructing twig furniture. In North America, the blue gum eucalyptus is generally found on the western border of California, south to Arizona and New Mexico, stretching along the Gulf Coast of Texas, and east to Florida. Because of its capacity to grow in semi-arid regions, blue gum euca-lyptus has been widely planted for windbreaks along dry fields.

GOLDEN CHINKAPIN (GOLDEN LEAF CHESTNUT) The golden chinkapin has leathery, oblong, evergreen leaves, two to five inches long, with smooth curled margins. Its flowers and burrs resemble those of chestnuts, but are smaller. On young trees the bark is smooth, and on older trees, it is broken into reddish-brown ridges.

The twigs and branches from young trees are useful for making the plant stands and garden tool carrier.

Where Golden Chinkapin Trees Grow

Golden chinkapins cluster along the western coast of North America from northern California to southern Oregon along the edges of pine and hemlock stands.

HAZEL Small trees or shrubs, hazel reaches heights of three to six feet. Its leaves are hairy, oval, or elliptical, and have a heart-shaped base and coarse, double-toothed margins. In the spring, the hazel's staminate catkins resemble those of birch, but its buds are oval and its fruit is a tiny nut enclosed by a leafy husk. In autumn, the leaves of the American hazel turn dull yellow, while the leaves of the beaked hazel (hazelnut) become bright yellow. Hazel twigs are dark brown, ranging from smooth on American hazel to rough on beaked hazel.

Hazel shoots are strong and its bark—which ranges from reddish-brown to yellowish-brown—is often densely hairy, lending a unique velvet appearance to twig projects. Supple young branches are useful for building trellises.

Where Hazel Trees Grow

American hazel occurs from Maine and Ontario south to Florida and Kansas. The beaked hazel tree grows from Nova Scotia to British Columbia, south to Georgia and Tennessee, and west from Kansas to Oregon. It grows in thickets, in moist or dry conditions and light soil, at the edge of woods or beside walls.

WITCH HAZEL   Witch hazel can be identified by its odd yellow flowers, which consist of four twisting petals, each about three-quarters of an inch long. The flowers appear in autumn and continue to hang on the bare branches after the leaves have fallen.

Witch hazel is most often used for small projects, such as the trellis planter.

Where Witch Hazel Trees Grow

Witch hazel is a small tree or shrub that grows in shady ground, and in the undergrowth of forests throughout the eastern half of the United States and Canada and as far south as Texas.

HICKORY   Hickory has often been called the most durable of native American hardwoods. In fact, when twig furniture manufacturing became a commercial venture in 1899, the Old Hickory Furniture Company chose hickory as its sole wood, and even today continues to manufacture hickory furniture in the traditional manner. Hickory is most commonly used for joined furniture (with a mortise and tenon structure) as opposed to my nailed-together designs, which are much easier for the novice.

Hickory bark is usually smooth and grey when young, becoming irregular with age. Its frayed edges give it a shaggy appearance. There are 11 hickories native to North America that can be used for twig furniture. The shagbark hickory has a distinctive, shaggy bark composed of thin, narrow scales that curve outward at the ends. Shellbark hickory resembles shagbark, but its leaves are very long, from 15 to 20 inches. Mockernut hickory has fragrant leaves that are eight to 13 inches long, with hairy stalks and narrow leaflets. Pignut hickory has a scaly bark that forms diamond-shaped ridges on mature trees, while bitternut hickory is distinguished from pignut by its smooth, grey bark. Water hickory produces leaves with reddish, hairy stems. Black hickory is easily recognizable because of its deeply furrowed black bark and its dark, reddish-brown nut. Nutmeg hickory's bark is scaly and reddish-brown, and its dark green leaves are often silvery-white on their lower surfaces.

Hickory saplings can be grown in a coppice, which is a woodland planted to yield a continuous harvest of twigs. Supple young branches are useful for trellis work, while larger pieces work nicely for chairs and shelves.

Where Hickory Trees Grow

Shagbark, shellbark, and black hickories grow on low hillsides and river bottoms, while pignut, mockernut, bitternut, and nutmeg grow in dry highlands. Water hickory is found along river swamps from southeastern Virginia to Florida and west to Texas. Most hickories grow throughout eastern and central North America.

CALIFORNIA LAUREL (OREGON MYRTLE)

California laurel has leaves that resemble the eastern mountain laurel, but they are broader ovals and smell like bay rum. It has a greenish-brown bark, either smooth or scaly, and is most often considered a shrub rather than a tree. California laurel is very hard when dry, and so is superb for building sturdy furniture.

Where California Laurel Trees Grow

California laurel grows along the extreme west coast in Oregon and California.

MADRONE (ARBUTUS)

This branch of the heath family is made up of more than 1,500 species growing in acid soils. Most are shrubs, and all have simple and—in most varieties—alternating leaves. Blueberries, rhododendrons, and heathers are familiar varieties of the heath family. Madrone can be easily recognized because of its thin, red-brown bark. Its wood is soft, and becomes hard and brittle when dry. Limbs two inches in diameter are useful for making chairs and tables, but smaller twigs should be soaked in a bucket of water and stored in a cool place until they are ready for use (usually within a week). Madrone's terra-cotta colored bark is particularly beautiful, and useful for trellises, the topiary standard, and the picture frame shelf.

Where Madrone Trees Grow

The Pacific madrone grows along the northwestern coast, from British Columbia as far south as San Diego, California, Texas and Arizona madrone trees grow in their respective regions, and are quite similar in appearance to the northern ones. Sourwood is a variety that occurs in Louisiana, Georgia, Tennessee, and the Carolinas. Lyonia grows throughout Florida and has a reddish-brown, usually scaly, bark that forms ridges on a twisted trunk.

MULBERRY   Mulberry belongs to a family that includes osage orange, commonly used for making archery bows. Two herbs, hop and hemp, are also included in the mulberry family. The three species most commonly used for building rustic furniture are red mulberry, Texas mulberry, and osage orange. Red mulberry produces deciduous leaves that are three to five inches long and two to three inches wide. It grows to heights of 60 feet, and its leaves turn yellow in the fall. Texas mulberry is similar but smaller, growing to only 15 feet in height. Its leaves are usually only an inch long. Osage orange produces multi-veined, deciduous leaves between three and five inches long, which turn bright yellow in autumn. Often used for hedge plantings, osage orange is distinctive because of its thorny twigs.

Mulberry twigs are useful for many projects, such as trellises, fences, chairs, and plant stands. Close-grained osage orange is hard and strong, and once its thorns are clipped, it is useful for almost all rustic projects.

Where Mulberry Trees Grow

Red mulberry grows in rich woodlands throughout Ontario, New York, and Vermont, from Minnesota to South Dakota, and from Florida to Texas. Texas mulberry, as its name implies, occurs as a small tree or shrub throughout the state and in the arid southwestern areas of North America. Osage orange can be found throughout most of the south and central portions of North America. It can be easily identified by its greenish-yellow bark and rough, inedible fruit, which ranges from three to five inches in diameter.

SWEETGUM   In the summer, sweetgum can be identified by its five-lobed, star-shaped, aromatic leaves. During autumn, these bright green leaves turn a brilliant red and gold. Its fruit is easily recognizable by its long stem and woody, burl-like head about one-and-a-half inches in diameter. The sweetgum's bark is scored with grey to brown ridges.

Where Sweetgum Trees Grow
Sweetgum grows in wet soils from southwestern Connecticut and southern New York to southern Missouri and eastern Texas. It is found as far south as central Florida.

PACIFIC   The leaves of Pacific dogwood resemble those of flowering dog-
DOGWOOD   wood but are larger, about four to six inches long and two to three inches wide. Its bark ranges from dark brown to black and is usually smooth, with scaly plates clustered around the bases of large trees. Pacific dogwood's showy white petals usually number six instead of the four found on the eastern dogwood.

   Twigs and branches of Pacific dogwood can be substituted for beech or any other eastern hardwood.

Where Pacific Dogwood Trees Grow
Pacific dogwood grows at low elevations in shaded, coastal areas of western North America from British Columbia to San Francisco.

WILLOW   Last but not least, willow is the most important wood for making rustic twig furniture. Luckily, the tree (shrub) grows throughout most of North America, and there are more than 100 rapidly growing species in the northern hemisphere. Because willow hybridizes in nature, true identification is often impossible, but it is also not necessary for our purposes.

All willows have long, thin leaves that are slightly notched, and catkins with varying amounts of silky fuzz. Early spring pussy willows can be found along frozen rivers in many areas, where a few branches may be gathered and brought into a warm house to "force" the sight of spring. Pussy willows can also be found standing in bunches at city florist shops at a time when the snow has become a grimy March blanket. (Purchased willows can often be used for small projects such as miniature chairs.)

All willow is pliable when green, and its flexible twigs create the warped, sculpted style of most rustic twig furniture. Its strength and flexibility are invaluable for scallop edging and wattle fencing. Most rustic craftspeople rely on willow for arbors and trellises where bending is required. Willow has a long history—the North American Indians used young willow shoots to fashion baskets, fish traps, and cradle carriers. Willow shoots usually remain flexible for up to two weeks after harvesting, but it is a good idea to soak the shoots in a bucket of water in a cool place until you are ready to use them. Permit yourself a few tries at bending them before beginning your project. Do not rush the bending and arching—slow and steady is the key here. With a little practice the novice can soon become an expert.

Where Willow Trees Grow

Willow usually grows along streams and creek beds, and in places where the soil is moist. Because most types of willow are similar, it is not necessary to identify each species. However, for those of you out on a willow-hunt in various parts of the country, I would like to mention some of the North American willows. In the western portions of the United States there are the Pacific willow, feltleaf willow, scouler willow, and hooker willow. The peachleaf willow grows throughout the south-central portion of the United States, as do the sandbar willow and the yewleaf willow. Balsam willow, bog willow, sage willow, and pussy willow are the most common willows of eastern North America. Diamond willow and hoary willow grow throughout most of North America in bogs and lowlands. Some of the finest willow in the world comes from areas where long growing seasons, cool nights, sunny days, and rich damp soil create ideal growing conditions for long straight shoots.

Willow roots easily, and is often planted in coppices. The most common, fast-growing tree, willow provides shoots during its first year that are excellent for making baskets, and a full twig crop suitable for making furniture during its third and fourth year. To plant willow for future harvesting, cut 12-inch lengths of willow shoots and plant them 10 inches deep, 18 inches apart in rich soil, preferably along a creek bed. In three to four years, a good willow crop for making twig furniture will be ready to harvest. Willow requires pruning to permit young shoots to grow; it is nature's way of recycling!

Peeled Willow

While bark is left on for almost all twig pieces, some craftspeople are experimenting with peeled willow work. It is usually best to peel the willow in the spring and summer months when the trees are growing and the cells beneath the bark are dividing rapidly. Cut the willow poles before peeling. Using a sharp knife, score a line down the length of the pole through the bark, and the "skin" should slip off. If not, carefully pry the bark loose with your fingers. Smooth, barkless willow, the color of a Kansas wheat field, has the look of natural wicker.

CHAPTER 2

Basic Methods for Working with Twigs

THE FIRST REQUIREMENT, OF COURSE, IS WOOD. Chapter 1, Finding the Wood, will tell you how to locate raw materials in your area. Try to find branches with interesting markings and unusual shapes, as they will help inspire your imagination and add uniqueness to your finished work.

Although most books on the subject suggest that wood should be cut in the winter to preserve the bark, I have not found this to be true, and have cut twigs in the spring and fall that have retained their bark as well. If, however, you want to strip the bark, cut in the summer when the trees are growing and the cells between the bark and the wood are dividing.

TOOLS AND EQUIPMENT You will need the following tools and equipment to build your garden twig furniture:

A crosscut hand saw, coping saw, single bit axe, garden shears, and/or clippers will be necessary for gathering the twigs.

A ⅜-inch variable-speed drill (electric or cordless is best—using an old-fashioned hand drill will take a little longer to finish your project) with a selection of bits; a hammer; and galvanized flathead nails in #4p, #6p, #8p, #10p, #12p, and #16p sizes are required to assemble the pieces of your project. You will also need a marking pencil, measuring tape or ruler, safety glasses, and work gloves. (Always use safety glasses or goggles when working with wood to shield your face and eyes from flying wood chips and sawdust.)

Optional Tools and Supplies

You may also need some of the following:

- For finer projects, ¾-inch finishing nails.
- A crosscut saw or key-hole saw.
- A cordless drill or hand drill for working on location.
- A ⅜-inch reversible drill if available.
- A drift punch (10 to 12 inches long) or a pocket knife for some projects.
- A 12-gauge wire and a wood chisel, and a two-inch rubber mallet.
- Linseed oil and turpentine or polyurethane if a piece is to be used out-of-doors for prolonged periods of time. A spray bottle or electric airless sprayer for applying the linseed oil/turpentine mixture.

Workbench

There are probably as many different types of workbenches, or work stations, as there are woodworkers. The simplest benches (and often the best) are heavy planks of wood standing on four legs. The legs are usually connected by rails that help to brace them, and perhaps support a few shelves. Dried 2′ × 4′ hardwood boards can be glued, or nailed together to create a suitable width for your work area. Attach this top with nails, or nuts and bolts to 4′ × 4′s for the legs. Location and area help to determine the size of your workbench, as well as your personal woodworking style. It depends on what is comfortable for you. I have seen workbenches in a variety of widths, lengths and heights. While some craftspeople choose to stand at a waist-high bench, others enjoy working on a knee-high version, where they are able to straddle the bench.

Many rustic furniture builders like to work outdoors, and don't have any use for a conventional workbench. Very often just a standing log is all that is required to help support a work-in-progress. One woodworker I know uses the open back of an old jeep as a work table, and moves his wood supply indoors to a heated basement to work on an old butcher block when the weather turns too cold. Rustic furniture can be built at the finest store-bought bench, but more importantly and in keeping with the spirit of the material, it can be built in the woods, in the garage, or at the kitchen table.

CHOOSING AND STORING BRANCHES

Always gather more branches than are required. Some of the lengths, diameters, and shapes you choose in the woods will not be suitable for the particular piece you are planning to build. It is a good idea to have a supply on hand.

Always gather more willow or other pliable branches than you need. It is not unusual to break a few during bending, especially when you are first getting started.

After each piece is cut, identify the part with a small slip of paper taped to the branch. This will help you quickly identify each branch as you assemble the project.

Fresh, green branches are suitable for all projects. Seasoned (dry) branches are suitable when bending is not required, especially for making chair and table legs. Only green branches can be used for the bendable parts. For best results, use fresh willow or vines within a few days of cutting. If this is not possible, stand the willow twigs in a bucket of water, placed where they cannot freeze. They can last for several weeks if you remember to keep the bucket filled with water. In order to keep vines supple, coil them into a wreath shape and submerge in a bucket of water with rocks placed on top of them to weigh the coil down.

BUILDING
THE PROJECT

After the wood has been gathered and the pieces selected and cut to size, assemble the basic frame structure, following the directions given. When the sub-assemblies are complete, it often helps to have someone hold the pieces upright while you connect the two sub-assemblies. The basic frame is then ready for the addition of the other pieces, such as arms, back, and seat. The bent willow is generally applied last. Here again it is a good idea to enlist an assistant to bend the willow (or alder) and hold it in place while you drill the pilot holes and nail the pieces together.

Checking for Strength and Safety

When your project is complete, check the stretchers, rails, and all other connecting beams for strength. This is especially important for chairs. Turn your finished piece over, and try to move the connecting members to ensure that the joints are secure. The joints should not wobble or move. At this point, if there is play in the joints, you may have to add extra nails, being sure to drill pilot holes first.

About Nails

Flathead galvanized nails are used for most of the joinery. Their subtle grey coloring blends in nicely with most wood tones, while their broad, flat heads ensure a firm joint. Galvanized nails do not rust and their rough surfaces hold well in both green and seasoned wood.

Finishing nails with small heads (sometimes called panel nails) are used for attaching thin twigs, usually the decorative elements.

Nails are sized in terms of pennies (#p), originally signifying the price per hundred. A #2p nail is one inch long, a #4p is one-and-a-half inches long, a #6p is two inches long, and so on.

Keep an assortment of galvanized nails near your work area. When you select a nail for each joint, make sure that it is just a little shorter than the combined thickness of the two twigs you are joining. The drill bit you use should be slightly smaller in diameter than the nail you plan to use. Drill each hole to a depth that is three-quarters of the length of the nail. You want the nail to bite firmly into the second member of the joint.

Use branches as braces for strength and rigidity. Add the braces front-to-back and side-to-side to keep the piece from swaying. They should form a triangle with two of the perpendicular branches of the piece—for example, leg and cross beams, or leg and side rails. When selecting branches for braces, remember that forked pieces are decorative while still being functional.

After the piece is completely assembled, it is a good practice to inspect all the joints and add nails where necessary to strengthen the assembly. An additional nail is usually required where a beam, a rail, and a leg meet, so that three nails are used at the joint.

Pilot Holes

Drilling holes before nailing (called pilot holes) will keep the wood from splitting as it dries. Select a bit that is slightly smaller in diameter than the thickness of the nail you are using. Pilot holes should be snug and shorter than the nail by about three-eighths of an inch.

Butt Construction

When project directions call for butt construction, it simply means that the end of one member fits flush against the other to form the joint.

BARK AND VINE PROJECTS   Although each type of natural material has its own unique uses, to my way of thinking nothing is as versatile as tree bark. Throughout history, bark has been put to use in a variety of ways. Birch bark is the most commonly used, as its natural waxes make it waterproof. It is also very durable and remains in the soil after the tree's inner wood has rotted away. Many cultures have developed uses for bark. Native Americans used the tough bark of the white paper birch to cover the twig frames of their wig-wams, and fastened large sheets of it over wooden frames to make canoes. They also made birch bark containers and, throughout the late 1800s and into the twentieth century, created birch bark souvenirs for the tourist trade. The Laplanders use bark to make plates and circular boxes, as well as for roofing shingles. In Switzerland, a large musical instrument called an alphorn, up to 15 feet long, is made out of birch bark.

My first bark basket was an antique one that I bought in Northern Canada about 20 years ago. The vendor told me it was made by a Cree Indian in the 1800s. Its sturdy shape fascinated me, and I still marvel at its simple charm. The bark of the birch is reversed, so that the paper white is on the inside and the reddish hue of the inner bark is displayed on the outside. The bottom and the side closing are laced together with willow, and it has a bent willow handle. This basket has delighted me throughout the years, and has served to hold fresh or dried flowers (with a glass jar inside), French bread at a buffet dinner, and a heap of pine cones and red ribbons during the holidays.

My second experience with bark took place in North Carolina, where I discovered an Appalachian berry basket. This unique basket is folded from one piece of bark, and its cylindrical shape and the concave eye-shaped base are its distinctive features. I have seen similar baskets made by the Cherokee, and assume that the early mountaineers learned from them how to make this basket.

WORKING WITH BIRCH BARK

Bark taken from freshly cut trees is usually pliable enough to use within a day or two. If, however, you have to wait several days before you begin your project, it is a good idea to soak the bark in water. A walk through the woods will often lead you to pieces of naturally peeled bark that you can use for some of the projects.

BARK WOODS

Paper white birch, black birch, cedar, chestnut, box elder, eucalyptus, hickory, palm, tulip poplar (yellow poplar), white walnut, yew, mountain magnolia, ash, linden, and bass are all good barks to use for projects. Alder and fir might also be usable. It is a good idea to experiment with bark from local trees to see which are appropriate for projects.

PEELING THE BARK

Use only bark from recently fallen trees. Do not peel bark from living trees. Stripping the bark from live trees will cause the tree to die.

To peel the bark from the branch, score a deep line lengthwise through the bark with a sharp knife. Make two cuts around the branch, marking the section of the bark to be removed. Place the top of a chisel along the scored line and gently tap it with a mallet. Continue until the section of bark is removed. If the project requires pressed bark, press the bark between heavy books or large flat rocks or bricks until ready to use. Depending on where you are comfortable working, pressing the bark can be done indoors or outdoors. Although I have successfully peeled bark during all seasons, it is easiest in the summer when the sap is up.

VINES

Those pesky bramble vines that often infest suburban yards and smother trees and bushes in the wild are another fine source of material. There is an almost limitless supply growing along roadsides. In addition, pruning some of these vines enhances the surrounding countryside.

GOOD VINES FOR PROJECTS

Bittersweet, Boston ivy, clematis, grapevine, honeysuckle, ivy kudzu, Virginia creeper, and wisteria (ivy and grape) are vines that are easy to use. Blackberry and raspberry are useful too, but must be dehorned.

CHAPTER 3

Fencing, Trellises, & Arbors

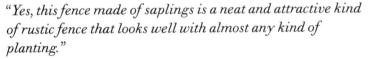

Wattle Border Fence

"Yes, this fence made of saplings is a neat and attractive kind of rustic fence that looks well with almost any kind of planting."

THE JUNIOR GARDEN CLUB OF AMERICA,

BETTER HOMES & GARDENS, JULY 1933

THIS ARRANGEMENT OF WOVEN TWIGS IS REMINISCENT of the fences devised by early settlers to separate their property and border their gardens. Wattle fences are fast becoming a versatile favorite of home gardeners, offering limitless possibilities by varying the rows of weaving. Three or four flexible shoots interlaced with slender twigs makes a charming natural edging for a low-growing herb garden, while the taller version can support a wall of sunflowers or climbing roses. A portable wattle fence adds instant drama and is a good backdrop for potted house-plants moved outdoors during warm weather.

MATERIALS
Skill Level: intermediate (short version), experienced (tall)
Willow, alder, mulberry, hickory, or any pliable branches are suitable. Choose sturdy branches for the posts and flexible saplings for weaving. The number of branches required depends on the size of the area you plan to enclose.

TOOLS
- Single bit axe for felling trees
- Crosscut hand saw
- Clippers or garden shears
- Ruler or measuring tape
- Marking pencil
- Sharp pocket knife
- Draw knife (optional)
- Drill and a selection of bits (optional)
- Safety gloves
- Work gloves

DIRECTIONS
The Edging
You will need straight branches 12" long, with ¾" to 1 ¼" diameters for the posts, and ½" diameter pliable saplings, as long as possible, for the weaving. It is best to arrange the branches and build the edging in the garden near where the finished fence will stand. The number of branches required depends on the size of the area you plan to enclose.

1. Using a sharp pocket knife, sharpen the ends of the posts.
   In soft ground, the posts can be hammered directly into the earth with the aid of a rubber mallet, or dig post holes spaced 8" to 12" apart with a sharp garden trowel. Install an *uneven* number of posts, or when you reach the end of the first row, you will have to go in front of or behind two neighboring posts.

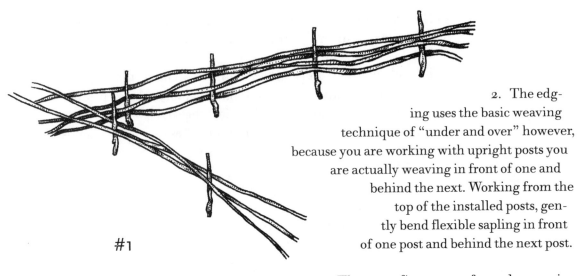

#1

2. The edging uses the basic weaving technique of "under and over" however, because you are working with upright posts you are actually weaving in front of one and behind the next. Working from the top of the installed posts, gently bend flexible sapling in front of one post and behind the next post.

Three to five rows of wattle weaving provides an attractive edging for ground-hugging plants.

The Border Fence

You will need straight branches 4' to 6' long, with 1" to 1 ½" diameters for the posts, and ½" to 1" diameter flexible branches, as long as possible, for the weaving. While it is easier to install the posts and do the weaving on site, it is possible to construct this version in the workshop and install it after it is complete. For on-site construction, the number of posts required depends on the area you plan to fence. A workable workshop size is 3' wide and 4' to 5' high.

Sharpen the post ends with a sharp pocket knife or a draw knife. If you are working on-site, hammer an uneven number of posts directly into the earth, 10" to 15" apart, with the aid of a rubber mallet or maul. Continue with the weaving technique described in step 2 (edging procedure) above.

Portable Wattle Fence

This interpretation places the branch posts in a split log base. You will need a log with a diameter of 6" to 8", 5' to 8' long. If you don't have access to logs of this dimension, contact a saw mill, and have one split in half at the mill. With the split side down, use a drill and bit to drill holes large enough to fit the upright post branches snugly. Drill holes approximately 12" apart. Refer to the diagram and place the upright branch posts in the base of the split log. Repeat the edging directions, above, for wattle weaving.

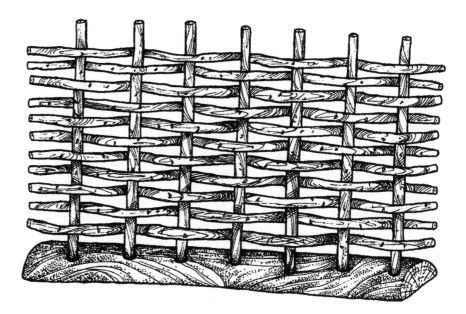

#2

Scallop Edging

"The loveliest flowers the closest cling to earth."
— JOHN KEBLE

THIS SIMPLE EDGING FENCE IS PERFECT FOR THE HERB or flower bed where low-growing blossoms like to trail and peek out through the horseshoe loops. It can be made in any length and its portable construction makes it handy to install along raised-beds, or a garden path.

Skill Level: beginner
Use woods such as willow, beech, cedar, hickory, or mulberry. You will need two straight poles, 82" long and 1 ½" to 2" in diameter for the rails; three straight poles, 7" long and 1" in diameter for the braces; and two straight poles, 18" long and ¾" in diameter. MATERIALS You will also need a selection of pliable branches, such as willow, alder, mulberry, or cedar for the horseshoe arches. Galvanized

flathead nails in assorted sizes and 1" finishing nails will also be necessary.

TOOLS
- Single bit axe for felling trees
- Crosscut hand saw
- Garden shears or clippers
- Ruler or measuring tape
- Marking pencil
- ⅜" variable-speed drill and a selection of bits
- Hammer
- Sharp pocket knife
- Safety goggles
- Work gloves

CUTTING CHART

Name of Part	Quantity	Diameter (inches)	Length (inches)	Description
Rails A	2	1 ½–2	82	straight/hardwood
Braces B	3	1	7	straight/hardwood
Stakes C	2	¾	18	straight/hardwood
Horseshoe arches D	6	¼–½	27	pliable

DIRECTIONS

Cutting the Branches

1. Cut two 1 ½" to 2" branches for the rails A, each 82" long.
2. Cut three 1" diameter branches for the braces B, each 7" long.
3. Cut two ¾" diameter branches for the stakes C, each 18" long.
4. Cut six ¼" to ½" diameter pliable branches for the horseshoe arches D, each approximately 27" long.

#1

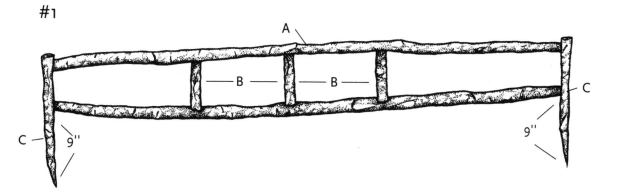

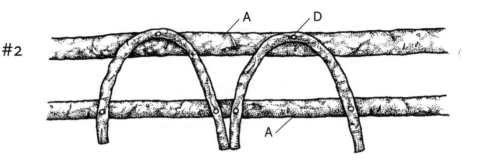

#2

Building the Basic Edging

1. Arrange the two rails A on the workbench. Using a pencil, mark the mid-point at the center of each rail (41"). The braces will be attached to the rails at these marks.
2. Mark two points at 15" right and 15" left of the mid-points on both rails.
3. Butt the center brace B, between the two rails A at the mid-point mark. Drill a pilot hole through rail A into B from the top, and nail in place. Turn the construction over and drill another pilot hole. Nail through A into B as before.

Adding the Stakes

1. Butt one stake C against both rails, allowing 9" to extend past the bottom rail. This sharpened end is inserted in the ground. Drill pilot holes and nail stake C in place through the top and bottom rails from the outside.

Adding the Horseshoe Trim

1. Gently bend one horseshoe twig D. Refer to the drawing and arrange one end of D against the bottom rail A. Drill and nail D in place where it meets the bottom rail; arching it along the top rail A, drilling and nailing in place to the top rail; and bringing it down and attaching it to the bottom rail with pilot hole and nail construction.
2. Repeat with the remaining horseshoe arches.

The Garden Gate

"*Sure she's the girl you used to
swing down by the garden gate.*"

DEAR OLD DONEGAL, A TRADITIONAL
IRISH TUNE

IT TAKES MORE THAN FLOWERS, HERBS, AND VEGETABLES
to establish a beautiful garden, and I can't think of anything
more appropriate than the addition of the quintessential garden
gate. Here is a rustic gate, perfect in almost any setting. It is designed to function as a swinging entry when installed between

fence posts, but its whimsical twig lettering offers a decorative element and it is perfect anchored in the garden among the scented cowslips, parsley, and lemon balm.

MATERIALS

Skill Level: intermediate

Use any hardwood such as beech, birch or cedar. Lengths will range from 29" to 42" and with 1" diameters for the gate frame. Three forked branches (any hardwood), 35"–42" long and ½"–1" in diameter will be needed for the brace trim. Use pliable shoots (willow or alder) for the lettering. You will also need galvanized flathead nails (#2p, #3p, #4p, #6p) for the gate and ¾" finishing nails or tacks for the letters.

TOOLS

- Single bit axe for felling trees
- Crosscut hand saw
- Clippers or garden shears
- Ruler or measuring tape
- Marking pencil
- Hammer
- Drill with a selection of bits
- Safety goggles
- Work gloves

CUTTING
CHART

Name of Part	Quantity	Diameter (inches)	Length (inches)	Description
Side supports A	2	1	42	hardwood
Stretchers B	2	1	29	hardwood
Top beam C	1	1	29	hardwood
Brace trims D (1,2&3)	3	½–1	35–45	forked hardwood

DIRECTIONS

Cutting the Branches

1. Cut two 1" diameter branches for side supports A, each 42" long.
2. Cut two 1" diameter branches for the stretchers B, each 29" long.

3. Cut one 1" diameter branch for the top beam C, 29" long.
4. Cut three forked branches with diameters from ½" to 1", and lengths from 35" to 45" for the brace trim D.

Building the Gate

1. Begin construction from the bottom. Butt the bottom stretcher B between side supports A. Drill pilot holes and nail stretcher in place from the outside of A.
2. Add top stretcher B in the same manner.
3. Butt top beam C between the side supports A, and with pilot hole and nail construction join together from the outside of A.

Adding the Brace Trim

1. Lay the construction face down on a flat surface. Overlap the middle forked brace trim D-1 on the top stretcher B, along the back. Butt the bottom single stem of the forked brace against the bottom stretcher B. Drill pilot holes through forked brace D, and bottom stretcher B. Nail in place using galvanized nails.

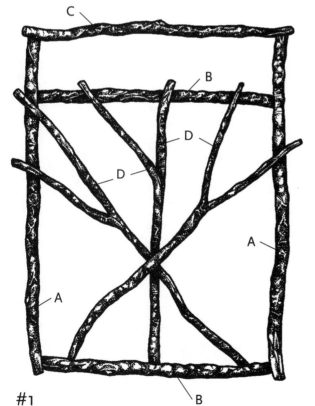

2. Diagonally overlap brace trim D-2, on the left side-support A, with the end butting against the bottom stretcher B. Attach to parts A and B with pilot hole and nail construction.
3. Repeat with remaining brace trim D-3, and nail in place.

#1

Adding the Lettering

The letters are formed with pliable twigs. The G is made up of five parts, nailed together using four thin finishing nails. It could also be made like the E which is formed by bending a supple twig into a U-shape and attaching the center line with a finishing nail. The same technique is used to form the A.

The R is made up of three parts, the D of two, and N is one supple twig with two bends.

Arrange the letters between the top stretcher B, and the top beam C, trying to keep them evenly spaced. Once satisified with the placement, using thin finishing nails, nail the letters to the top stretcher and the top beam, B and C.

Willow

Fan

Trellis

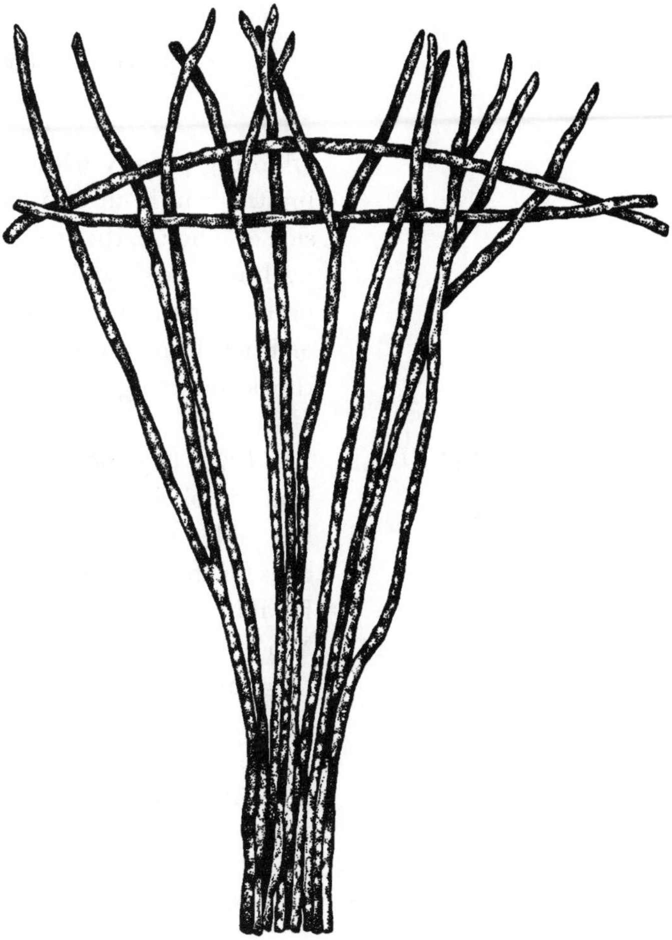

"April's air stirs in
Willow-leaves,
A butterfly
Floats and balances.

BASHŌ,
16TH CENTURY HAIKU

THIS SIMPLE FAN TRELLIS RETAINS THE TRADITIONAL look of its lattice cousin, while encouraging all manner of climbers to grow along its spreading branches. Once you master this easy technique you will probably want to make it in various sizes for specific locations. Equally at home in town or country, the willow fan trellis makes a perfect window or porch screen,

37

affording privacy while letting in light. Set in front of a wall or the side of a house, the trellis supports trailing vines, while helping to protect clapboards, ancient stones, or brick from invasive and sometimes damaging tendrils.

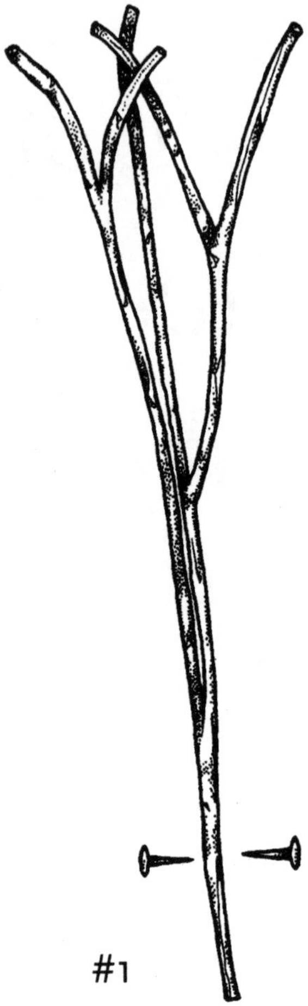

MATERIALS

Skill Level: beginner
Use any pliable twigs such as willow, alder or hazel; the sturdiest ones for the uprights and the more flexible for the horizontal weavers. You will need eleven uprights 62" long, and ¼" to ½" in diameter. You will also need two horizontal weavers 45" long and ½" in diameter. An assortment of galvanized nails is required.

TOOLS

- Single bit axe for felling trees
- Crosscut hand saw
- Clippers or garden shears
- Ruler or measuring tape
- Marking pencil
- Drill with a selection of bits
- Hammer
- Safety goggles
- Work gloves

#1

CUTTING CHART

Name of Part	Quantity	Diameter (inches)	Length (inches)	Description
Vertical uprights	11	¼–½	62	pliable
Horizontal weavers	2	½	45	pliable

DIRECTIONS *Cutting the Branches*

1. Cut eleven ¼" to ½" diameter branches for the vertical uprights, each 62" long. NOTE: Try to include some forked branches as shown in the illustration.
2. Cut two ½" diameter branches for the horizontal weavers, each 45" long.

Assembling the Trellis

1. Place the middle three vertical uprights together, side-by-side, on a work surface, making sure the ends are even.
2. Drill pilot holes part way through the three uprights, approximately 6" from the bottom, and nail in place as shown in diagram 1.
3. Add two more vertical uprights to both sides of the three previously joined uprights. With pilot hole and nail construction, add the two to the three as shown in diagram 2. You now have five joined uprights.
4. Add the remaining six uprights, three on either side, using pilot hole and nail construction, as shown in diagram 3.

Fanning out the Trellis

1. Interlace one horizontal weaver over and under the joined uprights at the

#2

top end, fanning the pliable verticals as you go. Repeat the weaving with the second horizontal twig continuing to gently fan the verticals. The force of the horizontal weavers should be enough to maintain the fan shape.

Hints for training vines around the trellis:

Some vines may require a bit of help to encourage them to cling to the trellis uprights. Tie them loosely with soft twine or yarn so as not to damage the tender shoots.

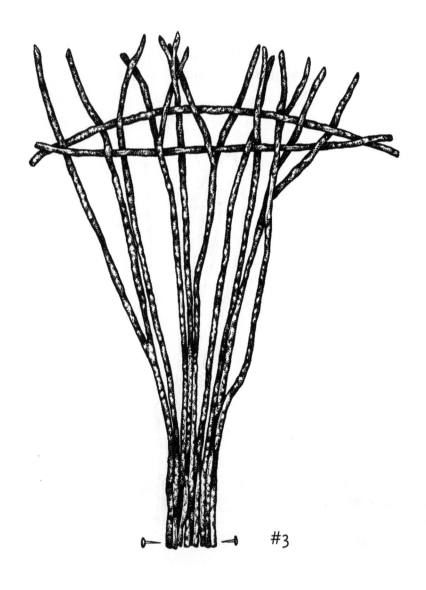

#3

Simple Trellis
& Trellis Arbor

"*Here canopied reaches of dogwood and hazel,*
Beech tree and redbud fine-laced in vines,
Fleet clapping rills by lush fern and basil … "
ANNE SPENCER

IT'S EASY TO CREATE INTERESTING GARDEN ARCHITECTURE
with this plain and natural design. One trellis is the perfect support for training climbing plants, deciduous or evergreen, an-
nual or perennial. By the simple addition of two braces to three
structures an arbor is created to help extend the landscape or

serve as a garden centerpiece. For a dramatic departure from the usual flowering vines, try growing hops along these rustic branches for a distinctive autumn display of dainty golden cones.

MATERIALS

Skill Level: beginner

Use wood like birch, cedar, hazel, maple, mulberry, or willow. To build one trellis you will need two 1 ½" diameter straight branches, 80" to 90" long; and five ¾" to 1" diameter branches, 26" to 36" long. Galvanized flathead nails in assorted sizes (#4p, #6p, and #8p) are used to join the elements.

TOOLS

- Single bit axe for felling trees
- Crosscut hand saw
- Clippers or garden shears
- Ruler or measuring tape
- Marking pencil
- Drill with a selection of bits
- Hammer
- Safety goggles
- Work gloves
- Pocket knife (optional)

CUTTING CHART

Name of Part	Quantity	Diameter (inches)	Length (inches)	Description
Side supports A	2	1 ½	80–90	straight
Overlap beams B	5	¾–1	26–36	straight

DIRECTIONS

Using a pencil and ruler, mark the points where the overlap beams B will be added to the side supports A to form the structure. Place the bottom beam approximately 10" up from the bottom of both legs. The top beam is placed approximately 12" down from the top of both legs. Each beam extends approximately 8" beyond the side supports. Adjust all measurments to suit your location.

Drill pilot holes through the overlap beams and partway through the side supports; nail in place using galvanized nails.

To create the simple trellis arbor, build three constructions (as above) with identical dimensions. Rest one trellis on the two top overlap beams to form the roof; nail in place with pilot hole construction. Angle two cross braces along the inside planes, between the roof side supports and the standing side supports.

The arbor is simply three trellises—two trellises in their upright (vertical) position, joined by one horizontal trellis, placed on top as a roof, connected with two cross braces.

A note on training vines:

Vines growing on arbors need to grow horizontally as well as vertically, and very often become extensions of their supports. A bit of training may be required, and you will want to be gentle with the young shoots. Sometimes all that is required is a simple arrangement, for the sticky tendrils soon take hold. For thicker branches, such as rose canes or grape vines, it is best to tie them loosely with soft twine.

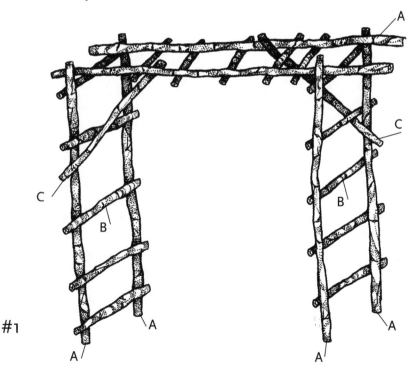

#1

Arched &
Vine-Wrapped
Arched Trellis

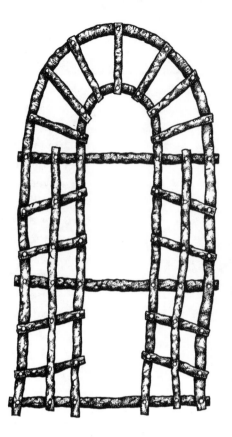

Rise; and put on your Foliage, and be seene
To come forth like the Spring-time, fresh and greene.
ROBERT HERRICK

MAKE AN ARCHED TRELLIS TO HELP TRAIN TRAILING RUGOSA
roses for summer fragrance and you will be treated to an en-
chanting tangle of autumn rose hips. By altering the placement
of two or three of these structures you will be able to add a dramatic dimension to your outdoor setting which promises year-
round interest. Spring offers tender shoots, and summer lush and
plentiful blossoms. Winter too has its special appeal in the gar-

den when rabbits and birds feed on seed pods left attached to trellis branches.

MATERIALS
Skill Level: beginner

Use woods like birch, beech, cedar, hickory, or willow. Lengths should range from 9" to 80" and diameters from ½" to 1 ½". A selection of pliable branches, as long as possible, ½" to 1" in diameter, will be needed for the arched top. Gather an assortment of supple vines, such as grapevine, for the vine-wrapped arched trellis. Galvanized flathead nails in assorted sizes (#4p, #6p, and #8p) and finishing nails (¾") will also be required. The arched trellis is 36" wide and 72" high. Heavy gauge copper wire may be required for lashing short parts together.

TOOLS
- Single bit axe for felling trees
- Crosscut hand saw
- Clippers or garden shears
- Ruler or measuring tape
- Work gloves
- Drill with a selection of bits
- Hammer
- Safety goggles
- Work gloves

CUTTING CHART

(Vine-Wrapped Arched Trellis Cutting Chart follows)

Name of Part	Quantity	Diameter (inches)	Length (inches)	Description
Overlap beams A	3	1–1 ½	36	straight
Braces B	15	½–1	12	straight
Side supports C	2	¾	44	straight
Center arch D	1*	½–¾	124*	pliable
Basic arch E	1*	¾–1 ½	156*	pliable

*NOTE: These are the exact measurements, but it is unlikely that you will be able to locate one usable, pliable twig with this diameter and length. See options #1, #2, and #3 for additional construction techniques.

DIRECTIONS

Cutting the Branches

1. Cut three 1" to 1 ½" diameter branches for overlap beams A, each 36" long.
2. Cut fifteen ½" to 1" diameter branches for the braces B, each 12" long.
3. Cut two ¾" diameter branches for the side supports C, each 44" long.
4. If possible, cut one ½" to ¾" diameter branch for the center arch D, 124" long; or cut two straight ¾" diameter branches 44" long, and one pliable ¾" diameter branch approximately 40" long.
5. If possible, cut one ¾" to 1 ½" diameter branch for the basic arch E, 156" long; or cut two straight ¾" diameter branches 60" long and one pliable ¾" diameter branch 64" long as shown in option 2; or cut two pliable branches, each approximately 82" long as shown in option 3.

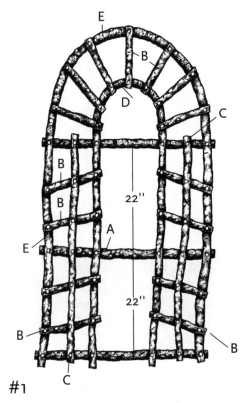

#1

Laying Out the Basic Framework

1. Construction begins with the basic arch, part E. With your gathered materials close at hand, decide on your construction technique.
2. NOTE: All beams A, *overlap* across the basic arch E. (Option 1): The beams are spaced equally, approximately 22" apart from where the arch begins to curve. Drill pilot holes through the three overlap beams A and the basic arch E at the points where they join (see diagram). Nail in place using galvanized nails.
3. (Option 2): In this model the basic arch is formed with three parts, two side supports C, and one center arch D. Drill pilot holes through the three overlap beams A and the basic arch E, at the points where they will join (see diagram). Nail in place using galvanized nails. Gently bend a pliable ¾" diameter

Option 1

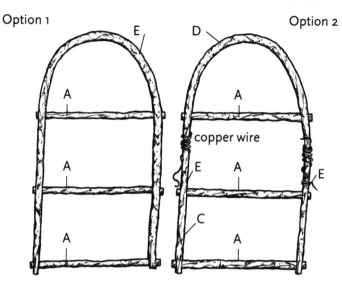

Option 2

#2

branch, approximately 40" long to form the top arched piece of E; join the ends of this arched piece to the sides of E by lashing them together with copper wire. NOTE: Copper wire weathers to a nice green patina and blends in perfectly with outdoor rustic work. Add the remaining overlap beam to the construction, spaced approximately 24" down from the arch.

4. (Option 3): In this example the basic arch E is formed with two separate branches, each approximately 82" long, which are lashed together, using copper wire, at the top. Add the three pre-drilled overlap beams, spaced approximately 22" apart as shown in the illustration.

Adding the Center Arch and Side Supports

1. The center arch is attached to the three overlap beams using pilot hole and nail construction in the same manner as the basic arch. Using one, two, or three branches, form the center arch and nail in place.

Option 3

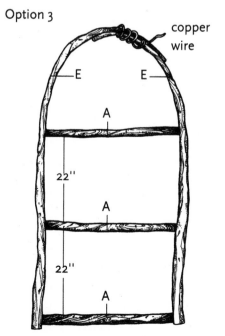

#3

2. Center the side supports between the basic arch E, and the center arch D, and nail, from the back, to the overlap beams, with pilot hole and nail construction and galvanized nails.

Adding the Braces

1. NOTE: The braces are spaced approximately 8" apart from each other. Using two nails for each brace, with pilot hole and nail construction, nail each brace, from the front, to both arched members, the center arch D and the basic arch E. Follow the arched shape of the top, and the braces will form a fan-shape as they are installed.

CUTTING CHART

Name of Part	Quantity	Diameter (inches)	Length (inches)	Description
Overlap beams A		*same as arched trellis*		
Braces B	8	½–1	12	straight
Side supports C		*same as arched trellis*		
Center arch D		*same as arched trellis*		
Basic arch E		*same as arched trellis*		

DIRECTIONS

Follow the cutting directions for the Arched Trellis, but you will only cut eight branches, ½" to 1" in diameter, and 12" long for part B. You will also be required to cut enough ½" to 1 ½" diameter supple vine to wrap around the structure. Vines are easy to twist and wrap when they are fresh, and surprisingly strong when

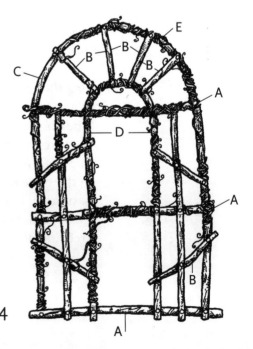

#4

they dry. They are very good for keeping your trellis straight and plants like to cling on the natural curly-cues and tendrils.

Follow the directions above for *Laying Out the Basic Framework*, and *Adding the Center Arch and Side Supports*.

Adding the Braces and Wrapping the Vine

1. Attach four braces B, in a fan-pattern from the basic arch to the center arch using pilot hole and nail construction and galvanized nails. Affix the remaining four braces B, diagonally from the basic arch to center arch, in the section between the overlap beams.

2. Interlace slender pliable vines over and under all parts; continue to weave and wrap the vines until you are satisfied with the arrangement.

#5

Pair of arched trellises

#6   Vine-wrapped trellis centered between two arched trellises

Cage Trellis

*"Habits and customs differ,
but all peoples
have the love of flowers in
common."*

CHINESE PROVERB

THE DENSE HEART-SHAPED LEAVES
of the exciting Moonflower (Ipomoea alba) and its giant
trumpet flowers seem made for this 34" tall cone-shaped trellis.
Its 17" diameter bottom easily fits over an 18" flowerpot or into a
24" pot. Well proportioned for the small terrace or deck, this
moveable three dimensional trellis is just as practical indoors
supporting a trailing plant.

MATERIALS   *Skill Level: intermediate*
You will need a piece of any kind of scrap lumber, approximately
¾" thick and 25" × 25" to make the pattern board to begin the

50

weaving. The trellis requires twelve ¼" diameter pliable twigs, 34" long; and six ¼" diameter pliable twigs, 24" long. You will also need a selection of ⅛" to ¼" diameter supple branches (or vines) for the weaving. Use whatever branches and vines are available to you. The easiest branches to work with are long and supple, such as first year saplings and spring and fall vines. Local vine, such as grapevine, wisteria, or kudzu may be used for the weaving. If you are using vines,

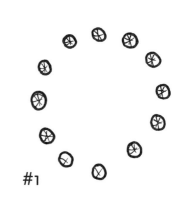

#1

gather them in the warm weather, and strip them of their leaves; weave the vines while they are still green (fresh). When they dry on the cage they will be very durable. If you must use winter vines, soak them in warm water to make them supple. Have 2 to 3 feet of string or wire handy to begin the weaving.

TOOLS
- Garden shears or clippers
- Drill with a selection of bits
- Marking pencil
- Carpenter's compass
- Ruler or measuring tape

DIRECTIONS

1. Place the lumber for the pattern board on a work table. See diagram 2. Using the pencil and carpenter's compass center a 17" diameter circle on the board. Mark off eighteen circles evenly spaced 3" apart. Drill

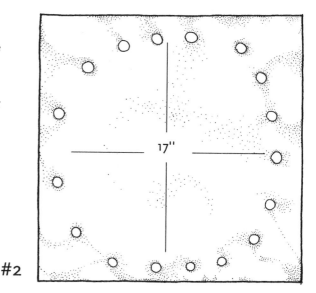

17"

#2

eighteen ¼" diameter holes, at the marks, approximately ½" deep. These holes hold the spokes in place during weaving.

2. Arrange twelve 34" long twigs (spokes) in *every other* pattern board hole. Gather the 12 spokes together at the top (see diagram 1), forming a 3" diameter, and loosely tie together with string or wire for a temporary hold. Begin weaving 2" from the top. Tuck one end of a twig or vine weaver in front of one stake and behind the next, and continue over-and-under, in front of one stake and behind the next until you have completed 6 or 7 rows. Tuck the ends of the weaver under and over itself to secure. The string may now be removed, or left in place until the project is completed.

3. Begin the second weaving section approximately 5" down the spokes from the last row of weaving. Continue weaving as above for 8 to 10 rows.

4. Now add the six remaining 24" long spokes. Remove the construction from the pattern board. Insert one 24" spoke next to a 34" installed spoke, pushing up into 4 or 5 rows of the weaving from step 3. Repeat with every 24" spoke along *every other* 34" spoke. Gently flare the 24" spokes, and arrange all spokes in the 18 pattern board holes.

5. Begin the third weaving section approximately 8" down from step 3, this time weaving all 18 spokes. Weave 3 to 5 rows.

6. Begin the last weaving section approximately 9" down from step 5. Weave 4 to 6 rows. The trellis should remain standing in the pattern board until the green spokes and weavers dry, usually overnight.

#3

Topiary

Standard

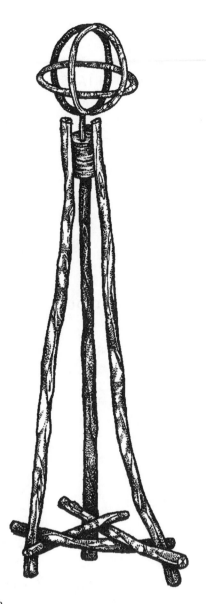

"Trailing odorous plants which curtain out the day with loveliest flowers"

PERCY BYSSHE
SHELLEY

CLIMBING TO THE TOP OF ANY gardener's list would be this easy to construct topiary form. Its well proportioned size makes it adaptable to a wide variety of climbing vines. Ivies, clematis, morning glories, nasturtium, thunbergia, and sweet peas are just a few of the plants you will want to try on this dramatic standard. Clinging tendrils and winding leafstalks attach themselves to the sturdy uprights while twining greenery is trained on the willow sphere.

MATERIALS

Skill Level: beginner

Any hardwood, such as birch, maple, hemlock, or mulberry ranging from 45" to 55" long and 1" in diameter is used for the basic structure. The legs splay outward, so be on the lookout for twigs with interesting crooks and bends at one end. The willow sphere is made up of three supple willow twigs, ¼" to ½" in diameter and 22" long. You will also need one ½" diameter twig, 4" to 8" long for the stem support, and one 1" diameter branch 3 ½" long for the spacer, as well as a selection of ¾" diameter branches at least 11" long for the stretchers. Copper wire is used to form the sphere.

TOOLS

- Single bit axe for felling trees
- Crosscut hand saw
- Garden shears or clippers
- Ruler or measuring tape
- Marking pencil
- Drill
- A selection of bits for Phillips-head drywall screws (1 ¼", 1 ⅝", and 2")
- Hammer and galvanized flathead nails (optional, to be used in place of screws)
- Finishing nails
- Wire clippers
- Safety goggles
- Work gloves

CUTTING CHART

Name of Part	Quantity	Diameter (inches)	Length (inches)	Description
Legs A	3	¾–1	55	birch, willow, or any green hardwood
Spacer B	1	1	3 ½	hardwood
Stem support C	1	½–¾	4–8	willow
Stretchers D	3	½–¾	11–14	hardwood
Sphere	3	¼–½	26	pliable

DIRECTIONS

Cutting the Branches

1. Cut three ¾" to 1" diameter green (fresh) branches, each 55" long for the legs A.
   NOTE: It is a good idea to use slightly tapered branches, with a bottom diameter slightly larger than the top diameter. These branches must be green and pliable in order to permit slight bending.

2. Cut one hardwood 1 ½" diameter branch, 3 ½" long for the spacer B.

3. Cut three branches ½" to ¾" in diameter and 11" to 14" long for the stretchers D.

4. Cut three supple twigs, such as willow or alder, each ¼" to ½" in diameter and 26" long for the sphere.

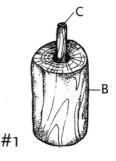

Building the Topiary

1. Mark the center of the 1 ½" diameter spacer B. Drill a hole completely through the spacer at the center mark, wide enough to accommodate the stem support C, keeping a snug fit.

2. Fit the stem support C in the spacer-drilled hole. Add a dab of glue if needed. Set the spacer aside.

#1

Drilling the Pilot Holes and Adding the Legs

1. Check each of the three legs to be sure they will fit properly against the spacer. Use clippers to remove any interference.

2. Mark a point from the top of a leg A, 1 ½" down, and then a second point approximately 2" down from the first. Butt the leg securely against the spacer B, leaving 1" to extend beyond part B. Hold leg firmly in place and drill at the two premarked locations, through the leg and part way through the spacer.

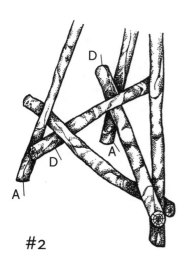

#2

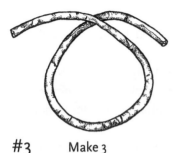

#3   Make 3

3. Using the correct Phillips-head drywall screw (or galvanized nails), attach leg A to spacer B.
4. Repeat the above steps with the remaining two legs.

Adding the Stretchers

NOTE: If you have crooks and bends located at a point 8" to 12" from the bottom of the legs, you will want to attach the stretchers at this point. Permit the wood to dictate the design. The stretchers D will be attached under and over each other, forming an equilateral triangle.

1. Drill a pilot hole approximately 1" to 1 ½" from the end of one stretcher D and through a point 8" to 12" up from the bottom of one leg. Using Phillips-head screws (or galvanized nails) attach the stretcher to the leg at this point.
2. Gently extend the second leg outward; attach the stretcher to the extended leg in the same manner as the preceding step.
3. To attach the second stretcher D, place one end of the second stretcher over the installed stretcher, and using pilot hole construction, attach to the same leg.
4. Attach the third stretcher over one installed stretcher and under the other.

Forming and Adding the Sphere

1. Form a ring with one of the 26" long pliable twigs, and secure the ends by wrapping them under and over each other as pictured.
2. Repeat the above step with the remaining two rings.
3. Fit the three pliable rings

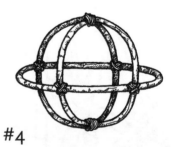

#4

into the sphere, and join together at their meeting points with copper wire.

4. Attach the sphere to the installed stem support C with two or three finishing nails.

5. Stand the topiary stand upright, and check to see if it stands straight. Use a sharp knife or clippers, if necessary, to adjust the ends.

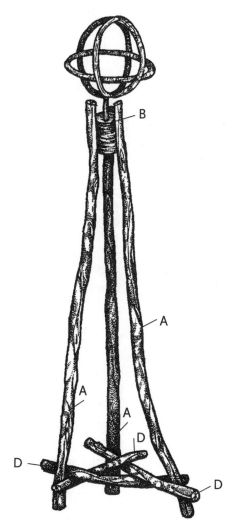

#5

Window Box Trellis

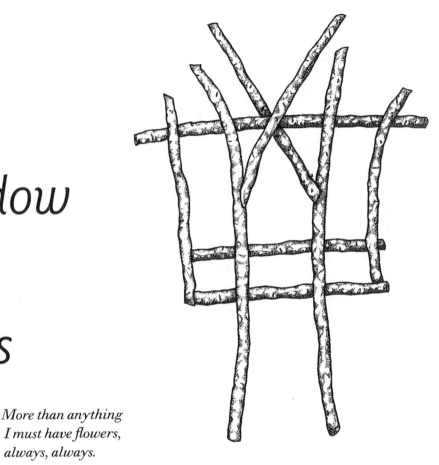

*More than anything
I must have flowers,
always, always.*

CLAUDE MONET

DESIGNED WITH ORDER IN MIND, THIS MINI TRELLIS IS
well suited for window boxes with seasonal blooms. An evergreen ivy would be a good trainer along the trellis branches in
most semi-protected window boxes. Allow the ivy to grow year
round, and plant blue hyacinths, purple pansies, and yellow
tulips for a springtime display. After blooming, replace the flowering bulbs with pink annuals such as geraniums or petunias for
the summer, and then with fluffy mums in the fall, always keeping the trellised ivy as a background plant. Winter boxes may be
filled with Irish juniper, white pine, or hemlock seedlings, sometimes found in the woods.

MATERIALS

Skill Level: beginner

I used willow and mulberry for this project, but any hardwood would work nicely. It's easier to work with the branches when they are green, but you could alter the design a bit if only seasoned twigs are around. Lengths range from 12" to 20", with all diameters approximately ½". Finishing nails are used to join the parts, and if your twigs are green you can probably avoid drilling pilot holes.

CUTTING CHART

Name of Part	Quantity	Diameter (inches)	Length (inches)	Description
Stakes A	2	½	20	pliable
Overlap beams B	2	½	12	straight
Side supports C	2	½	12	pliable
Cross braces D	2	½	12	straight
Top beam E	1	½	16	straight

TOOLS

- Hand saw
- Clippers or garden shears
- Ruler or measuring tape
- Marking pencil
- Drill (optional)
- Finishing nails
- Hammer
- Safety goggles
- Work gloves
- Pocket knife (optional)

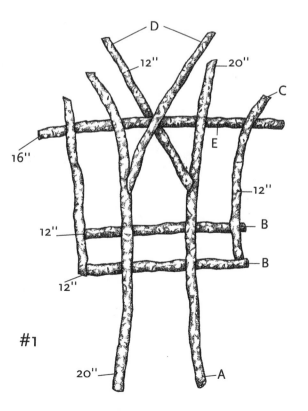

#1

DIRECTIONS   *Cutting the Branches*

1. Cut two ½" diameter pliable branches for the stakes A, each 20" long.
2. Cut two ½" diameter branches for the overlap beams B, each 12" long.
3. Cut two ½" diameter pliable branches for the side supports C, each 12" long.
4. Cut two ½" diameter branches for the cross braces D, each 12" long.
5. Cut one ½" diameter branch 16" long for the top beam E.

Assembling the Trellis

1. Place the two stakes A on a work surface and arrange them so that they are spaced approximately 7" apart. Mark a point 9" from the bottom of each stake A. Lay one overlap beam B across the stakes and nail at the points.
2. Place the second overlap beam B across the stakes in the same manner at a spot approximately 4" apart from the attached overlap beam. Drill (if necessary) and nail in place.
3. Place the sub-assembly face up on the work surface. Place the side supports C under the beams at the outside edges. Drill (if necessary) and nail in place.
4. With the front side up, lay the

#2

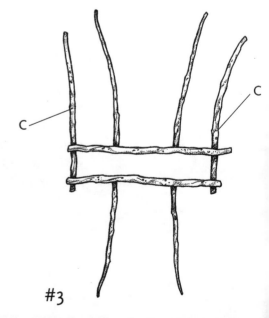

#3

top beam E over the stakes and the side supports at a location approximately 9" from the second overlap beam. Drill (if necessary) and nail the top beam to the stakes and to the side supports.

5. Fit the cross braces D along the stakes so that they cross at the mid-point of the top beam, beveling the ends as needed. Nail in place from the back.

Now that you have made the window box version, you may decide to try your hand at enlarging the design to build a full size trellis for the yard or porch screen.

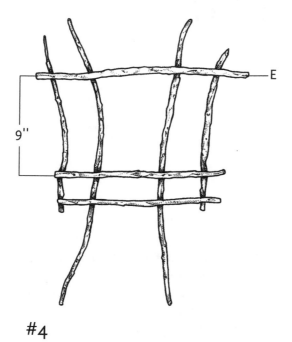

#4

Shelter Arbor (Cabana)

"Windyridge, let winds unnoticed whistle round your hill!"
SIR JOHN BETJEMAN

TWO EIGHT-FOOT STRUCTURES ARE JOINED WITH A ROOF made of forked branches to create this handsome walled arbor, perfect for wisteria vines. It can be a screen, or with awning canvas panels, it becomes a sheltered nook. Add a bench for garden gazing or pond side viewing. The first step in designing your version is to decide where it will be located. The measurements given here seem to work well for individual sections. Two or more sections may be joined to fit your needs and the site. Make it portable or stationary, permanent or temporary.

MATERIALS *Skill Level: experienced*

You will need 2" and 3" diameter hardwood branches, from 28" to 96" long. Pliable willow shoots ½" to 1" in diameter, and approximately 85" long are required for the hoops and trim. Forked hardwood branches, at least 36" long are used for the roof. Galvanized flathead nails are used and some finishing nails may be required to attach thin willow shoots to the design.

TOOLS
- Single bit axe for felling trees
- Crosscut hand saw
- Clippers or garden shears
- Ruler or measuring tape
- Marking pencil
- ¾" variable-speed drill
- Hammer
- Safety goggles
- Work gloves

CUTTING
CHART

Name of part	Quantity	Diameter (inches)	Length (inches)	Description
Side post rails A	2	2	96	hardwood
Beams, B1, B2, and B3	3	1 ½–2	60	hardwood
Braces C	3	1 ½	30	hardwood
Horseshoe trim	5–8	½–1	80–90	very flexible
Roof	5, or more	¾–1 ½	36, or longer	forked, hardwood

DIRECTIONS
1. Butt the bottom beam B1 between the two side post rails A, approximately 5" from the bottom of the rails. Join with pilot hole and nail construction through the side of the post rail A.
2. Butt and join beam B2 in the same manner 30" up from beam B1.
3. Butt and join beam B3 in the same manner 5" to 12" down from the top of post rails A.

4. Butt the middle brace C at approximately 30" between B1 and B2. Join with pilot hole and nail construction drilling through the top of B2 and the bottom of B1.

5. Evenly space, and butt the remaining braces between the beams and join as above.

6. Gently bend and add horseshoe trim as pictured, or as desired. Very often the twigs have a mind of their own, and will dictate the design to you. Allow your imagination to run free when adding trims and loops and fanciful embellishments.

NOTE: The basic design may be adjusted, and another version spaces beams B1 and B2 20" apart, and calls for braces C to be 20" long.

To make the cabana, place two panels at right angles (more, or less), and join together with roof parts.

To set up the cabana outdoors, tap stakes in the ground and nail to the side post rails to keep the structure steady.

I'm sure you can think of many spots to place an outdoor cabana: near the pool or the pond, by the hot tub, in the herb garden, in a sheltered area up on the hillside, or out in the field behind the pumpkin patch. Use your imagination to adjust the basic design to create

#1

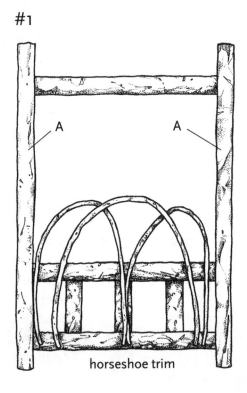

horseshoe trim

fences, gates, gazebos, and arbors. This project can be reshaped, and its branches shortened or lengthened to suit your needs.

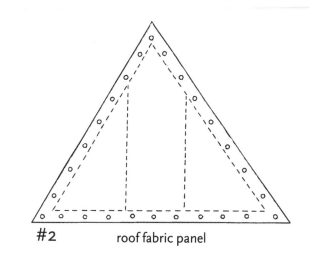

#2   roof fabric panel

MATERIALS TO COVER THE CABANA: 3–4 yards 54" wide water resistant canvas (or other suitable outdoor fabric, such as sun-and fade-resistant nylon) for the roof. 5 ½ yards 54" wide water resistant fabric for the sides. Grommet tool and grommets (available at sewing centers and hardware stores). 24 yards of rope (a clothesline works nicely).

DIRECTIONS: Cut fabric pieces. NOTE: Fabric for the roof section will have to be sewn together. All fabric parts will need a 1 ½" hem along the edge. Measure the sections to be covered. Add ½" seam allowance around all the pieces that make up the roof section and the side panels, if needed.

- Sewing and Hemming: Using ½" seam allowance, sew together the roof section. Sew a 1 ½" hem around the edge.
- Adding the Grommets: Attach the grommets with the grommet tool, spaced evenly approximately 6" apart, along the outside hemmed edge.
- Attaching the Fabric Roof: Using the rope, lace the roof section *inside* the cabana over and around the roof branches.
- Hemming the Side Panels: Sew a 1 ½" hem around all four sides of the side panels.

- Adding the Grommets: Attach the grommets with the grommet tool, spaced evenly approximately 6" apart along all four sides.
- Attaching the Side Panels: Using the rope, lace the side panels *outside* the cabana over and around the side post rails, A.

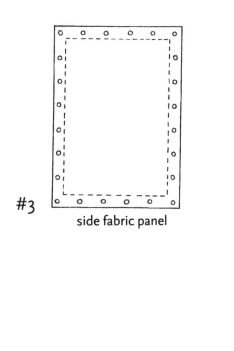

#3

side fabric panel

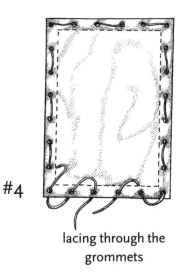

#4

lacing through the
grommets

The Summer House

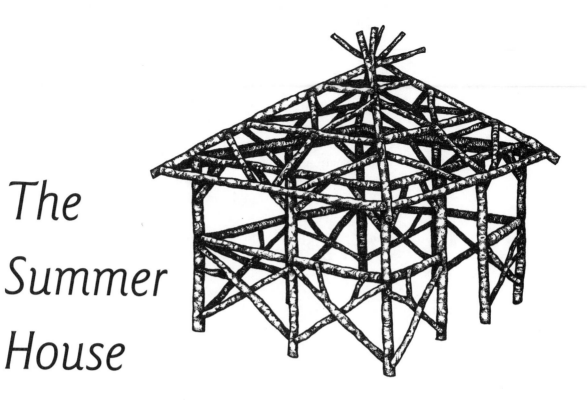

"When covered with running vines, the arbor becomes a canopy under which a seat may be placed in pleasant weather."

FRANK A. DE PUY, 1900

WHEN I BEGAN WRITING THIS BOOK, A FRIEND ASKED ME to help him design an outdoor room that he could use as an arbor to provide support for some native grapevines that he discovered growing wild on his property. He wanted me to design a large project he would be able to construct by himself, hundreds of miles away from my home. At first it sounded like a difficult assignment, but the rough sketches soon developed into a design that he felt comfortable with, and he foraged, purchased, and collected timbers from various sources. Armed with some basic construction techniques, a good selection of 2" to 4" diameter straight branches, a small chain saw, a power drill, and with some willing assistants, my friend built his rustic structure. Chairs and a small log table were placed inside, and the gnarled and ancient grapevine shoots were planted along the supports.

My friend is delighted with his outdoor retreat. It is his special resting spot on lazy summer afternoons.

MATERIALS   *Skill Level: experienced +*

The sides of the summer house are approximately 8' tall and 10' wide. Nine 8' straight branches, with 4" diameters make up the basic structure; the doorway is 3' wide. Eight 12' straight branches with 3" to 4" diameters are required for the basic roof structure. Eight 3" diameter straight branches are used for the cross rails, and 2" diameter branches for the diagonal braces. Pilot holes and rough-finished galvanized nails are used to connect the posts to the top beam.

Stainless-steel nails will not rust and you may decide to splurge and use them for this project. Countersunk lag screws are used to attach diagonal braces. NOTE: To countersink lag screws drill a pilot hole using a

#1

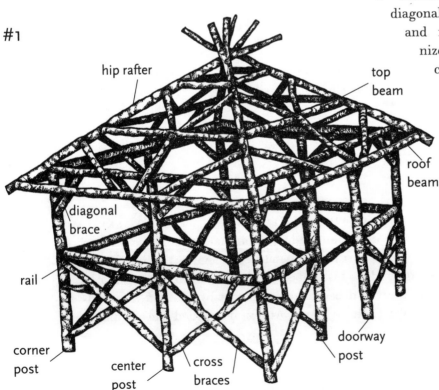

hip rafter

top beam

roof beam

diagonal brace

rail

corner post

center post

cross braces

doorway post

bit larger than the screw, or use a fluted counterbore to countersink the screws. Countersink holes should be deeper than the length of the screw. When all screws are driven, holes may be plugged with pegs, cut from branches.

TOOLS

- Single bit axe for felling trees
- Chain saw (optional)
- Crosscut hand saw
- Clipper or garden shears
- Ruler
- Marking pencil
- ⅜" variable-speed drill and drill bits
- Hammer
- Sturdy step ladder
- Plumb bob
- Level
- Safety goggles
- Work gloves

#2

roof section

#3

side section

#4

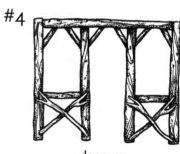

doorway

DIRECTIONS 1. It is important to begin with solid, straight poles for the posts to guarantee a straight and neat structure. Arrange each corner post plumb, at its desired location temporarily braced with two or three pieces of scrap lumber. These temporary braces hold the post in place while work begins on the structure.

#5

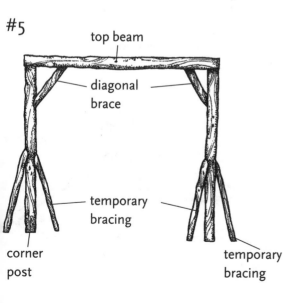

top beam

diagonal brace

temporary bracing

corner post

temporary bracing

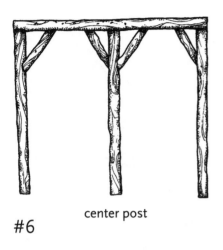

#6

center post

2. Assemble the beams on top of the corner posts and join together with nails. Add one, or two diagonal braces from post to top beam using a lag screw at each junction. These braces help to strengthen the structure.

3. Assemble the basic roof parts in place. Attach the roof beams to the hip rafters. Notice that the diagonal hip rafters extend and cross at the top. The roof beams extend approximately 12" beyond the corner posts. The roof will be filled in later with various braces.

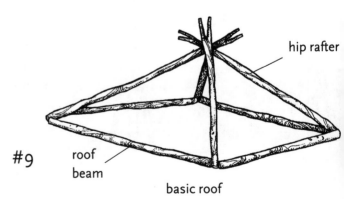

#8

4. Plumb the center post on each of the three sides, and join to the top beam with nails. Add diagonal braces from center post to top beam using countersunk lag screws.

5. Arrange the two doorway posts in place, at approximately 3 ½ feet from the corner posts, and attach to the top beam. Add diagonal braces.

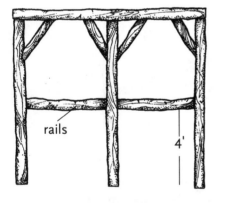

rails

4'

#7

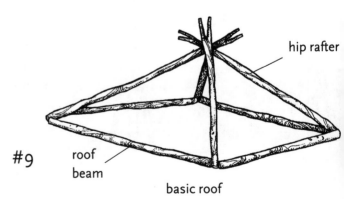

#9

roof beam

hip rafter

basic roof

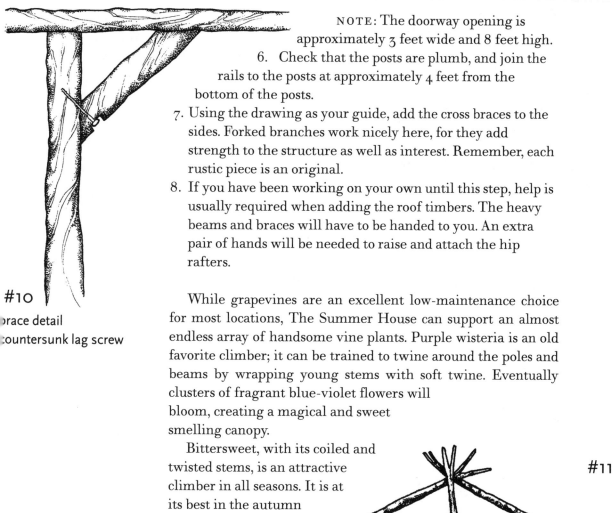

#10

brace detail

countersunk lag screw

NOTE: The doorway opening is approximately 3 feet wide and 8 feet high.

6. Check that the posts are plumb, and join the rails to the posts at approximately 4 feet from the bottom of the posts.

7. Using the drawing as your guide, add the cross braces to the sides. Forked branches work nicely here, for they add strength to the structure as well as interest. Remember, each rustic piece is an original.

8. If you have been working on your own until this step, help is usually required when adding the roof timbers. The heavy beams and braces will have to be handed to you. An extra pair of hands will be needed to raise and attach the hip rafters.

While grapevines are an excellent low-maintenance choice for most locations, The Summer House can support an almost endless array of handsome vine plants. Purple wisteria is an old favorite climber; it can be trained to twine around the poles and beams by wrapping young stems with soft twine. Eventually clusters of fragrant blue-violet flowers will bloom, creating a magical and sweet smelling canopy.

Bittersweet, with its coiled and twisted stems, is an attractive climber in all seasons. It is at its best in the autumn when its summer green leaves turn a clear yellow. When the leaves fall, tiny orange-yellow cap

#11

roof in place

#12

sules split and masses of orange-red berries are abundant. These vivid berries remain throughout most of the winter, where they contrast with the winter landscape. Bittersweet is a vigorous climber and will require trimming once established.

Hydrangea, trumpet vine, and clematis are rapid growing flowering vines that will wrap their way along the rustic sides and scramble across the twig roof. Or how about a rose-covered summer house? Be sure to take into account the location of your structure, as well as your temperature zone when seeking advice from a nursery or garden guidebook. If your summer house is in an exposed area, for example, it will probably be hit with an early frost. Whether or not you decide to add vines, your summer house is bound to be an attractive and welcome addition.

9. Each roof section requires at least two additional beams, and five braces. Decorative curving branches are nice for braces.

Braces help to make your structure strong and straight. Add more braces, if needed.

NOTE: The Summer House shown in the photo section is a variation on the directions provided here. The Summer House in the photo has a shingled roof and a solid wood floor, both of which are beyond the scope of this book. Remember that any of these projects can be changed or added to as long as you are comfortable with the basic design.

CHAPTER 4

Shelves

Lovers Retreat, Woodland, N. Y.

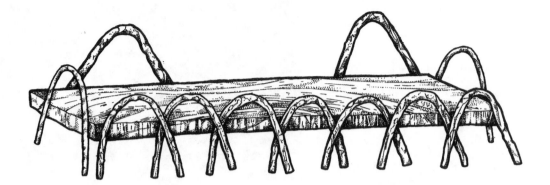

Hanging Plant Shelf

"A garden should be rather small,
or you will have no fun at all."
REGINALD ARKELL

GATHER UP YOUR PRIZE PLANTS AND SET THEM ON THIS willow-trimmed shelf. This versatile shelf is at home on a porch, along a picket fence, in a guest room, or on a kitchen wall. For old-fashioned charm, try weaving blue velvet ribbon through the willow loops and setting pots of lavender on the shelf. It makes a perfect perch for evergreen topiaries during winter celebrations. Attach it to the wall with sturdy pegs or hooks.

MATERIALS
Skill Level: beginner
You will need to use pliable branches such as willow, alder, or cedar. Lengths will vary from between 14" and 17", and branches should be ⅛" in diameter. A ½" thick wood plank, 4 ½" × 25" is required for the shelf. You will also need 1" finishing nails.

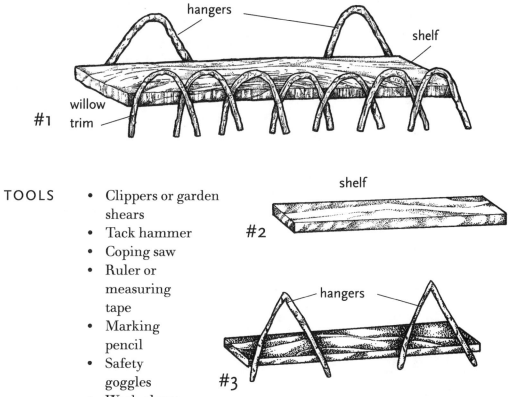

#1 hangers · shelf · willow trim

TOOLS
- Clippers or garden shears
- Tack hammer
- Coping saw
- Ruler or measuring tape
- Marking pencil
- Safety goggles
- Work gloves

#2 shelf

#3 hangers

CUTTING CHART

Name of Part	Quantity	Diameter (inches)	Length (inches)	Description
Hangers A	2	¼	17	pliable
Braces B	2	¼	5	pliable
Border trim	13	¼	14–17	pliable
Shelf	1	½" thick	4 ½ × 25	pine, or scrap wood

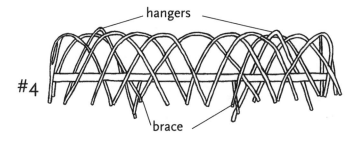

#4 hangers · brace

DIRECTIONS

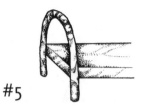

#5

#6

#7

#8

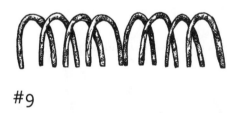

#9

1. Following the diagrams, step 1 through step 6, gently bend, arrange, drill, and nail each pliable twig in place, along the side and front shelf edge as illustrated, creating the border trim as you proceed. Any variation of twig border placement is possible.

2. Turn the construction over, and attach the hangers A to the back edge by gently bending each 17" long pliable twig in a "V" shape. Using pilot hole and nail construction, nail the hangers in place at approximately 2" from the outside edge.

3. Add the braces B, to the bottom end of the hanger part closest to the inside and the bottom of the shelf with pilot hole construction. The brace is an important element, adding stability and strength to the construction.

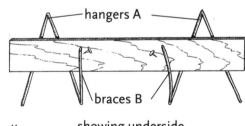

#10   showing underside

Picture
Frame
Shelf

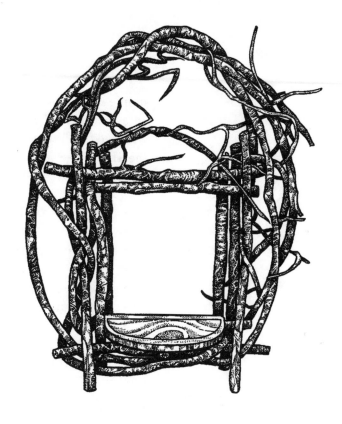

"A display of orchids is like a floral fancy-dress ball."
E. M. HARDINGE, 1894

THIS VIRGINIA CREEPER—WRAPPED FRAME SHELF WAS inspired by fragrant herbs and scented geraniums peeking out behind some discarded picture frames at an old farmhouse. It will provide support for a pot of trailing grape ivy resting on its shelf, or a vase of fresh picked garden flowers.

MATERIALS *Skill Level: intermediate*
Use such woods as willow, beech, or hickory for the basic frame. Lengths will vary from 14" to 22" with ¾" diameters. Two 18"

supple willow branches are needed for the shelf trim along with an assortment of green (pliable) vine for the frame wrap. You will need a 1" thick slice of lumber approximately 6" × 10" for the shelf. Use galvanized flathead nails in assorted sizes, and finishing nails (¾", 1", and 1 ½") for the assembly.

TOOLS

- Single bit axe for felling trees
- Hand saw
- Garden shears or clippers
- Ruler
- Marking pencil
- Drill with a selection of bits
- Hammer
- Safety goggles
- Work gloves

CUTTING CHART

Name of Part	Quantity	Diameter	Length (inches)	Description (inches)
Top/bottom rail A	2	¾	14	hardwood
Side rail B	2	¾	17	hardwood
Top/bottom rail C	2	¾	17	hardwood
Side rail D	2	¾	19	hardwood
Top/bottom rail E	2	¾	19	hardwood
Side rail F	2	¾	22	hardwood
Shelf brace	1	¼–¾	8–9	forked, hardwood
Shelf	1	1" thick	6 × 10 half-circle	pine board
Shelf trim	1–2	¼–1	18	pliable

Vine frame wrap: one, or two lengths of supple vine, as long as possible to wrap the frame. Use such vines as Dutchman's pipe, grapevine, honeysuckle, kudzu, and Virginia creeper.

DIRECTIONS

Cutting the Branches

1. Cut two ¾" diameter branches for the top/bottom rails A, each 14" long.

2. Cut two ¾" diameter branches for the side rails B, each 17" long.

3. Cut two ¾" diameter branches for the top/bottom rails C, each 17" long.

4. Cut two ¾" diameter branches for the side rails D, each 19" long.

5. Cut two ¾" diameter branches for the top/bottom rails E, each 19" long.

6. Cut two ¾" diameter branches for the side rails F, each 22" long.

7. Cut one ¼" to ¾" diameter forked branch for the shelf brace, 8" to 9" long.

8. Cut one or two ¼" to 1" diameter pliable branches for the shelf trim, 18" long.

9. Cut the supple vine to length as indicated on the cutting chart.

Assembling the Frame

1. Lay side rails F down 13" apart and parallel, on the workbench.

2. Using the marking pencil, make a mark 4" from each end of both F rails. Overlap one top/bottom rail E, at the 4" mark. NOTE: Approximately 2" of rail E will extend beyond rail F.

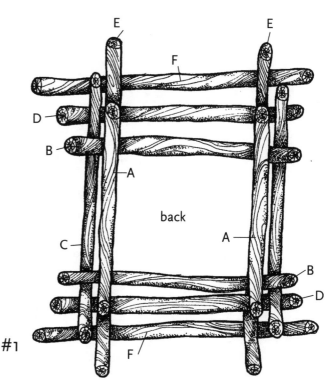

#1

3. Nail E to F with pilot hole and nail construction. Repeat with remaining E and F rails.

4. Overlap side rails D across side rails E, allowing approximately 2" to extend. Nail the D rail to the E rail as in step 3 above.

5. Overlap top/bottom rails C across side rails D, allowing approximately 2" to extend. Nail the C rail to the D rail as above.

6. Overlap side rails B across rails C, allowing approximately 2" to extend. Nail C to B as above.

7. Overlap top/bottom rails A across side rails B, allowing approximately 2" to extend. Nail A to B as above.

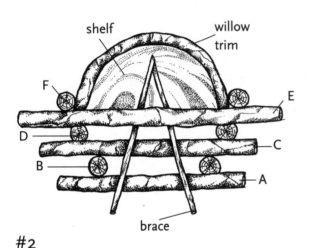

#2

Adding the Shelf

1. The half-circle shelf is nailed to the bottom E rail. Arrange shelf in place, and using pilot hole and nail construction, nail the shelf to the E rail from the back.

2. Position the shelf brace as shown in diagram 2. Join the brace to the bottom of the shelf and the bottom rail A, with finishing nails.

3. Gently bend the shelf trim around the outside edge of the shelf. Attach trim to shelf edge with pilot hole construction and finishing nails.

4. Refer to the drawing to wrap and weave the vine along the extended frame parts. At this point, the vine usually has a mind of its own, and somehow it finds its way along the extended branches.

Rustic

Etagere

"Ah, well September, the garden is still soft and green,
rinse out the flower pots, and get them clean."

MARY SCRIBNER, 1873

DESIGNED TO BE PRACTICAL AND STURDY, THE SHELF UNIT
is easy to construct with ¾" pine boards and 6' long poles. Once
you learn the technique, you will probably want to build a wall
of shelves, or combine several to fit any space. This 5' wide, 5' 8"
high unit is ideal in a potting shed, or outdoor protected area for

storing flower pots, potting soil, and harvest trugs, while the extended branches serve as hooks for hanging hand tools, garden gloves, and accessories.

MATERIALS
Skill Level: experienced

Seven ¾" pine boards, 5' long (the standard width for these is 6 ¾"). Three 1" × 4" boards 68" long for the back supports. Five hardwood (beech, birch, or maple) tree poles, in lengths ranging from 68" to 80" including extended branches, and ¾" to 2" in diameter. 2-inch to 4-inch galvanized nails are required. NOTE: The size of the nails is determined by the diameter of the poles. Phillips-head screws (2 ½" drywall) are used to join the back supports to the shelves.

TOOLS
• Single bit axe for felling trees
• Crosscut saw
• Clippers or garden shears
• Ruler or measuring tape
• Pencil
• Hammer
• Electric drill and bit to accommodate three Phillips-head screws, or a hand-held Phillips-head screwdriver
• Safety goggles
• Work gloves

CUTTING CHART

Name of Part	Quantity	Diameter	Length (inches)	Description (inches)
Shelves A	7	width 6 ¾	60	pine board
Back supports B	3	1 × 4	68	pine 1 × 4
Upright poles C	5	¾–2	68–80	hardwood branches

DIRECTIONS
Cutting the Shelves

1. With the crosscut saw cut all ¾" pine boards (shelves) to size. These can be cut to size at the lumber yard.

NOTE: Shelves may be left natural, painted, or stained as desired. If you choose to paint or stain them, do so before construction begins.

Building the Shelves

1. Lay the front lips of the shelves on the floor, spaced as follows:

top shelf
8"
9"
10"
11"
13"

Adding the Vertical 1" × 4" Back Supports

NOTE: The back supports are added to the shelves while the shelves remain spaced on the floor.

1. Arrange the center backboard B, vertically on top of all the back edges of the shelves A.
2. Using the drywall Phillips-head screws and the drill, attach the center backboard B to all of the shelves A, at the spot where they meet.
3. Repeat step 2 with the remaining two back supports.

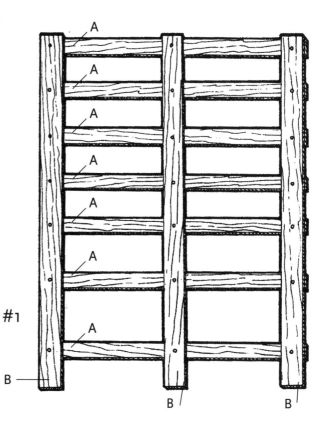

#1

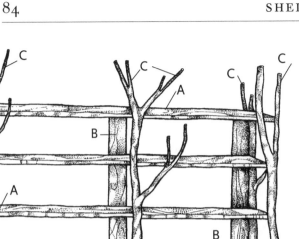

#2

Raising the Shelves and Adding the Twig Uprights

NOTE: At this point it is helpful to have assistance. Both of you will now raise the unit to its standing position. Have your helper continue to hold the unit steady as you proceed.

1. Arrange the front/center upright C along the front of the shelves as pictured. Make sure the pole easily touches each shelf at each junction point. When you are satisfied with the placement, drill pilot holes through the upright pole C, and each shelf at the points where they will be attached.
2. Using galvanized nails, join the upright pole C to the shelves.
3. Repeat with the right and left front upright poles C, as in step 2 above.
4. Arrange and attach the remaining right and left back poles C.
5. Clip all protruding lower branches.

Plant Whatnot

"When I pick or crush in my hand a twig of bay, or brush against a bunch of rosemary, or tread upon a tuft of thyme, or pass through incense-laden Cistus, I feel that here is all that is best and purest and most refined, and nearest to poetry."

GERTRUDE JEKYLL

MEMORIES OF GRANDMOTHER'S WHATNOT SHELVES combine with rustic twigs to create this shelf unit for displaying favorite plants. With its open shelves and corner design it can be used indoors near a window, or in any sheltered outdoor location. While you can probably find a spot for this piece almost anywhere, it seems just perfect for a kitchen corner where fragrant herbs can mingle with seasonal flowers and early spring seedlings.

MATERIALS

Skill Level: intermediate
You will want to choose straight branches for the legs and braces. Lengths will range from 14" to 50" and diameters from ¼" to 1 ¼". You'll need four pieces of ½" pine (or similar wood) for the shelves, each 14" × 20". You will also need a selection of galvanized box nails, #2p, #4p, and #6p, along with finishing nails. Sandpaper may be required for the shelves.

TOOLS

- Single bit axe for felling trees
- Crosscut hand saw
- Clippers or garden shears
- Ruler or measuring tape
- Marking pencil
- ⅜" variable-speed drill
- Hammer
- Sharp pocket knife
- Carpenter's level (optional)
- Safety goggles
- Work gloves

CUTTING CHART

Name of Part	Quantity	Diameter (inches)	Length (inches)	Description
Back leg A	1	1 ¼	50	straight, hardwood
Front legs B	2	1 ¼	46	straight, hardwood
Top beam C	2	¾	14	straight, hardwood
Bottom beam D	2	¾	14	straight, hardwood
Long braces F	2	½	36	straight, hardwood
Short braces G	2	¼–½	18	straight, hardwood
Brace trim H	8	¼	2 ¼–2 ½	straight, pliable
Shelf E1,E2,E3 & E4	4	see diagram	14 × 19 ½	½" pine

DIRECTIONS

Cutting the Branches

1. Cut one straight 1 ¼" diameter branch for the back leg A, 50" long.
2. Cut two straight 1 ¼" diameter branches for the front legs B, each 46" long.
3. Cut one straight ¾" diameter branch for the top beam C, 14" long.
4. Cut one straight ¾" diameter branch for the bottom beam D, 14" long.
5. Cut two straight ½" diameter branches for the long braces F, each 36" long.
6. Cut two straight ¼" to ½" diameter branches for the short braces G, each 18" long.
7. Cut eight straight, and pliable ¼" diameter branches for the brace trim H, each 2 ¼" to 2 ½" long. NOTE: Pliable branches are easier to install, and the lengths are adjusted during construction to ensure a tight fit.
8. Shelves are triangle-shaped ½" white pine measuring 19 ½" across the front and 14" along the sides. NOTE: Other woods such as walnut, cherry, or oak may be used for shelves. Cut the four shelves roughly to size, allowing an extra ⅛" all around for finishing. Lightly sand all shelves, if necessary.

Marking the Branches

1. Hold front legs B upright and choose an inside edge of each branch.

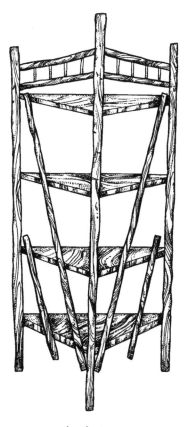

#1

back view

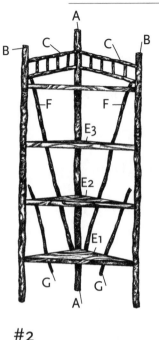

#2

2. On the inside edge of each leg B, make a pencil mark 8" up from the bottom of each leg.
3. Make another pencil mark 10" above the first marks. Continue to mark the branches, each 10" above the one before, until you have marked 4 locations along the inside edge of each front leg B.
4. Repeat steps 2 and 3 above along the inside edge of the back leg A.
5. On the inside edge of each front leg B, make a pencil mark 3 ½" down from the top of each leg.
6. On the outside edge of the back leg A, make two pencil marks 5" down.
7. Make another pencil mark 3" below the first marks on each front leg B (from step 5).
8. Make another two pencil marks 3" below the first marks on the back leg A.

Building the Stand

1. Use a sharp knife (or clippers) to taper the end of one top beam C to approximately one-third of its diameter. Butt C against leg A at the top pencil mark (5" down from the top) and check for a tight fit. Drill a pilot hole through the end of C and part way into A and nail C to A.
2. Butt top beam C against front leg B at the top pencil mark (3 ½" down from the top). Taper the end of C, as above. Check for a tight fit. Join C to B with pilot hole and nail construction.
3. Repeat step 1 with the second top beam C, on the opposite side against back leg A.
4. Repeat step 2 with opposite front leg B, remembering to use pilot hole and nail construction and nailing from the outside of the legs.
5. Butt one bottom beam D against leg A at the pencil mark 3"   #3

down. Taper the end, and check for a tight fit. Join D to A
with pilot hole and nail construction.

6. Taper, butt, drill, and nail one bottom beam D against front
   leg B at the 3" pencil mark.

7. Repeat with remaining bottom beam D on the opposite side.

Adding the Shelves

1. Beginning with the lowest shelf E1, arrange the 19 ½" side
   squarely between the two front legs B, and the back leg A at
   the first pencil marks, and check for a tight fit. Trim the shelf
   to fit, if necessary. Drill pilot holes through B and A at the
   pencil marks, and part way through the shelves, nailing only
   three-quarters of the way through. Leave one-quarter of the
   nail exposed until the construction is completely assembled.
   This prevents the driven nails from being loosened as you
   proceed.

2. Repeat step 1 above, fitting, drilling, and
   nailing the remaining three shelves in
   place at the pencil marks, working from
   the bottom up. Be careful when drilling
   and nailing, making certain that the
   shelves are level as you proceed.

Adding the Braces and Trim

1. With the back of the construction facing
   you, arrange one long brace F diagonally
   along the shelves, beginning
   approximately 5" from the bottom of the
   back leg A, slanted toward the top of the
   front shelf. The brace is installed to the
   edge of the top shelf approximately 2"
   from the front leg. See diagram. The long
   brace is attached to all four shelves at
   their junction. Repeat with the remaining
   long brace on the opposite side.

#4

2. Arrange one short brace G diagonally along the bottom two shelves, E1 and E2 as shown in the diagram. Attach H to the shelves as above. Repeat with the remaining short brace.

3. Evenly space pencil marks along the top beam C, approximately 3" apart. Fit brace trim pieces H, between the top and bottom beams at the 3" pencil marks. Trim H parts to fit if necessary. Drill and nail in place from the top of beam C, and through the bottom of beam D. Repeat on the opposite side.

Finishing

Hammer the exposed nails into place. Check the construction, and adjust the legs if necessary so that the shelves are balanced. Shelves may be left in their natural state or finished with linseed oil or paint. If you choose paint, it would be wise to paint before installation.

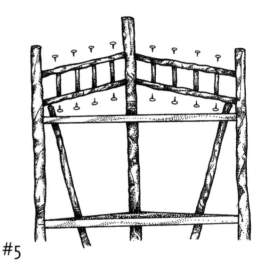

#5

Standing Box Planter

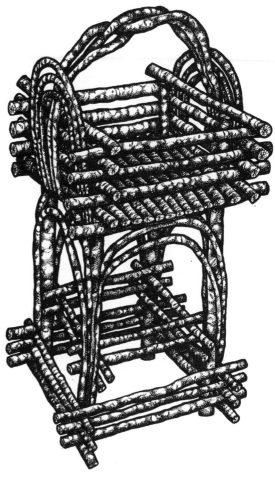

"Especially should a small garden, I think, be full of sweet scented flowers; it gives them a loveable, intimate quality."

LOUISE BEEBE WILDER

GARDEN CHARM IS PROMISED YEAR ROUND WITH THIS two level planter. Don't let the number of twigs frighten you. Learning these techniques will help you with larger projects, and hopefully inspire you to create your own designs. Cascading with dainty blooms, the standing planter is the perfect welcome beside any front door. Use its sturdy handle to carry it inside at the first sign of frost to brighten up a winter room.

MATERIALS *Skill Level: experienced*
You will need sixty ¾" diameter twigs, ranging in length from 15" to 18" for the basic structure; four 1 ¼" diameter branches, 28" long for the legs; and twenty-four ½" to ¾" diameter branches for the platforms. You will also need an assortment of ¼" and ½" diameter pliable branches, from 22" to 40" long for the horseshoe trim and the handles. Galvanized flathead nails in assorted sizes (#4p, #6p, and #8p) and about four dozen finishing nails will also be necessary.

TOOLS
- Single bit axe for felling trees
- Crosscut hand saw
- Clippers or garden shears
- Ruler or measuring tape
- Marking pencil
- ⅜" variable-speed drill
- Hammer
- Safety goggles
- Work gloves

CUTTING CHART

Name of Part	Quantity	Diameter (inches)	Length (inches)	Description
Legs A	4	1 ¼	28	hardwood
Top rails B	16	¾	18	hardwood
Lower rails C	10	¾	15	hardwood
Bottom staves D	12	¾	18	hardwood
Platforms E	24	½–¾	17	hardwood
Handles	3	½	40	pliable
Top horseshoe trim	6	¼	22–30	pliable
Lower horseshoe trim	4	½	40	pliable

DIRECTIONS *Cutting the Branches*
1. Cut four 1 ¼" diameter branches for the legs A, each 28" long.
2. Cut sixteen ¾" diameter branches for the top rails B, each 18" long.

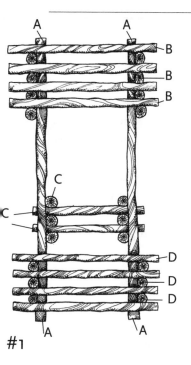

#1

3. Cut ten ¾" diameter branches for the lower rails C, each 15" long.
4. Cut twelve ¾" diameter branches for the bottom staves D, each 18" long.
5. Cut twenty-four ½" to ¾" diameter branches for the platforms E, each 17" long.
6. Cut three ½" diameter pliable branches for the handles, each 40" long.
7. Cut six ¼" diameter pliable branches each from 22" to 30" long, for the top horseshoe.
8. Cut four ½" diameter pliable branches for the lower horseshoe trim, each 40" long.

Laying Out the Sub-Assembly

1. The top rails are joined in the familiar log-cabin pattern at the top of the legs, by assembling alternating parallel branches at right angles.
2. With a pencil, make a mark 7" from the top of all four legs. Attach one top rail B to the leg A, at this point with pilot hole construction. Allowing 3" of the rail to extend beyond the adjoining leg, attach the rail to the next leg in the same manner, at the 7" mark. The legs should be 11" apart.
3. Repeat step 2 above with the remaining two legs and one rail.
4. Lay two rails B across the leg-attached rails, butting against the outside of the legs, to form a square. Nail to the leg from the outside.

Laying out the Top Platform

1. Arrange approximately eleven platform parts E across the two parallel rails, allowing about 2"

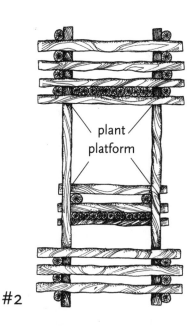

plant platform

#2

to overhang both rails. Using pilot hole and nail construction, nail the platforms to the rails at each junction.

Building the Box

1. Lay two top rails across the platform parts and the outside leg rails, butting against the legs. Nail to the rail beneath it at all four ends.
2. Lay two more rails, outside the legs, across the rails beneath, and nail in place, remembering to use pilot hole and nail construction.
3. Repeat the above procedure with the remaining 8 rails, nailing each branch to the one beneath it.

Building the Lower Rails and the Lower Platform

1. Turn the construction on its side so that the inside legs are visible. Overlap one lower rail C, across two legs at a location approximately 7" from the bottom. Drill pilot holes and nail in place.
2. Turn the construction over, and repeat with the opposite side.
3. Turn the construction up. Arrange approximately thirteen bottom platform branches across the two parallel lower rails C, allowing 2" to overhang both rails. Nail the platform branches to the rails at each junction.
4. Place two lower rails C, across the platform, *inside* the legs. Drill pilot holes and nail rails from the inside.
5. Continue to place remaining four lower rails across existing rails, inside the legs. Nail each rail in place to the rail beneath it.

Adding the Bottom Staves

1. Overlap one bottom stave D, across two bottom legs A (as close to the bottom as possible). Drill pilot holes and nail in place.
2. Repeat step 1 on the opposite side.
3. Lay one bottom stave D, across the just installed staves, on

side, with
handle and
bottom trim

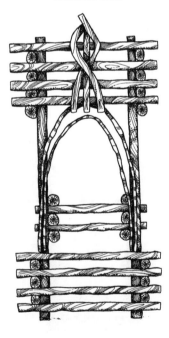

#3

the outside of the legs. Drill pilot holes and in place to the stave beneath it.

4. Repeat step 3 on the opposite side.
5. Continue to build, log-cabin fashion, with the remaining staves.

Adding Bottom Trim

1. Refer to the assembly diagram for the lower horseshoe trim placement. Gently bend one 40" pliable branch into an arch. Place one end against the outside of one leg and carefully bring it up, arching it and bringing it down along the leg on the opposite side, ending it just above the bottom stave. Drill and nail in place using thin finishing nails.
2. Repeat with the three remaining sides. NOTE: The lower horseshoe trim is applied to the four sides, while the top trim and the handle are attached to two sides.
3. To form the interior lower horseshoe trim, gently bend one 36" pliable twig, and using the same method as above, nail the horseshoe to the leg, just inside the attached horseshoe.

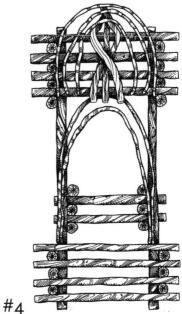

#4

side, adding handle and horseshoe trim

Adding the Handles

1. Gently bend one handle twig and place it against the outside of the (first-installed) top rail B, and bring it up along the other three, allowing it to arch approximately 25" at the top, bringing it down along the rails on the opposite side. Drill and nail in place to two or three rails on both sides.
2. Repeat with the remaining two handle parts, carefully wrapping them around the first handle.

Adding the Top Horseshoe Trim

1. Refer to the assembly diagram for the top horseshoe trim placement. To form the trim, gently bend each pliable twig in place, and using the same method described in *Adding Bottom Trim*, nail three horseshoe trims in place along the sides, and on top of the handles.

Window Box

"A little garden square and wall'd."
TENNYSON

IN THE PAST WINDOW BOXES WERE USED MOSTLY BY city dwellers, as a way to make a garden of the smallest porch or windowsill. Today, window box planters are used indoors as well as outside, adding color, texture, and scent to any number of settings. Filled with potted plants, this twig box is the perfect centerpiece for your picnic table, or heap it with vegetables for your harvest feast. To use it as a traditional window box outdoors, it will have to be supported on four sturdy brackets or rest on a shelf, if the window sill is narrow.

MATERIALS *Skill Level: beginner*
You will need 36 twigs of any wood, ranging in length from 8" to 25" with diameters from ½" to ¾" for the window box. You will

also need flexible ½" diameter branches, from 15" to 30" long for the horseshoe trim and the handles; and 1" finishing nails.

TOOLS

- Crosscut hand saw
- Garden shears or clippers
- Drill and bit
- Ruler
- Marking pencil
- Hammer
- Safety goggles
- Work gloves

CUTTING CHART

Name of Part	Quantity	Diameter (inches)	Length (inches)	Description
Front/back rails A	12	½–¾	22–25	hardwood
Side rails B	10	½–¾	8–11	hardwood
Bottom staves C	15–20	½–¾	8 ½	hardwood
Handles D	4	½	22–30	pliable
Horseshoe trim E	12	¼–½	12–18	pliable

DIRECTIONS

Cutting the Window Box Branches

1. Refer to the Cutting Chart and Assembly Diagrams. Mark the parts as you cut them to speed up the assembly process. A good way to do this is with a strip of masking tape that can be removed easily.

   All the following branch diameters are ½" to ¾".
2. Cut two 22" branches for the front/back rails A.
3. Cut two 22 ½" branches for the front/back rails A1.
4. Cut two 23" branches for the front/back rails A2.
5. Cut two 23 ½" branches for the front/back rails A3.
6. Cut two 24" branches for the front/back rails A4.
7. Cut two 25" branches for the front/back rails A5.
8. Cut two 8" branches for the side rails B.
9. Cut two 9" branches for the side rails B1.

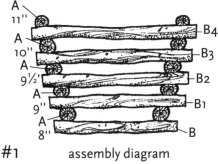

A
11"
A
10"
A
9½"
A
9"
A
8"

B4
B3
B2
B1
B

#1 assembly diagram
showing side rails B

10. Cut two 9 ½" branches for the side rails B2.
11. Cut two 10" branches for the side rails B3.
12. Cut two 11" branches for the side rails B4.
13. Cut fourteen 8 ½" branches for the bottom staves C.

Building the Bottom

1. The log-cabin design is built by alternating rails A and rails B; the slight variation in the size of the rails is required to create the window box shape.
2. Begin by laying both A rails down, parallel, on the workbench. At approximately 3" from both ends of the rails arrange the fourteen bottom staves C across the two parallel rails A. Nail staves to rails with pilot hole and nail construction.

Constructing the Box

1. Begin by laying one side rail B across the ends of the two parallel rails A. Nail in place.
2. Repeat on opposite side.
3. Lay one front/back rail A1 across the side rails B. Nail in place.
4. Repeat on opposite side.
5. Lay one side rail B1 across the ends of rails A1. Nail in place.
6. Repeat the above procedure until the remaining front/back rails, A2, A3, A4, and A5, and the remaining side rails, B2, B3, and B4 are nailed. The structure should flare out slightly as each layer is added.

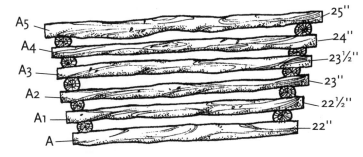

A5
A4
A3
A2
A1
A

25"
24"
23½"
23"
22½"
22"

#2

assembly diagram showing front/back rails A

Adding the Handles

1. Gently bend one 30" pliable twig. Place one end of the twig against the inside of both front/back rails A along the outside of the side rails B. Bring it up along the front/back rails, forming an arch at 5" above the side rail B4, and bringing it down along the inside edge of the A rails on the opposite side. Drill and nail in place where the handle meets the side rails, using thin finishing nails.
2. Repeat with the opposite side of the window box.
3. Using the same method as above, attach one 22" pliable handle part inside the attached handle, forming the double handle.
4. Repeat with the opposite side of the window box.

Adding the Horseshoe Trim

1. Refer to diagram 3 for horseshoe trim placement. To form the outside trim, gently bend one 18" pliable twig. Place one end of E against the inside of the bottom side rail B and bring it up along the front/back rails, arching it and bringing it down along the front/back rails on the opposite side, allowing it to rest inside a bottom stave C. Drill and nail in place using thin finishing nails.
2. To form the interior horseshoe trim, gently bend one 12" pliable twig, and using the same method as above, nail the horseshoe in place inside the attached horseshoe.
3. Repeat with the remaining horseshoe trims, creating three pair for each side.

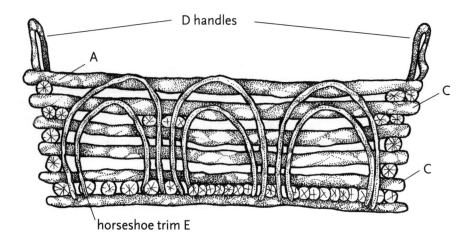

D handles

A

C

C

#3   horseshoe trim E

Trellis Wall Planter

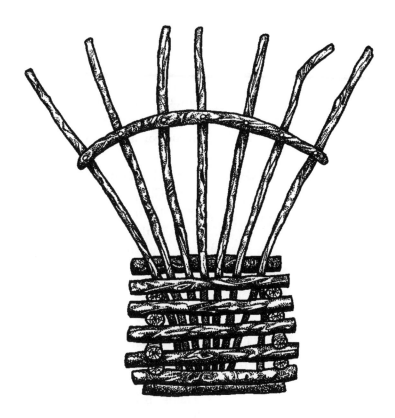

"Springtime is advancing up the valleys and slopes of the northern hills ... "
CALVIN COOLIDGE

SITTING ON A TABLE, OR HANGING ON THE WALL, THIS 10" square planter with attached trellis support is a dramatic accent to hold your favorite plants and flowers. It is perfect for ivy winding, as well as for trailing plants such as creeping fig, jasmine, or philodendron. Whether you use it for nasturtiums on the porch or creeping rosemary in the kitchen, you will probably want to make several.

MATERIALS   *Skill Level: beginner*
You will need 23 twigs of any wood, 10" long and ¾" in diameter for the planter. You will also need 8 pliable branches, such as wil-

low, each 24" long and ¼" to ½" in diameter for the trellis. Finishing nails or wire brads (finish nails without a head) are used in the construction.

TOOLS
- Hand saw
- Clippers or garden shears
- Drill and bit
- Ruler
- Pencil
- Hammer
- Safety goggles
- Work gloves

CUTTING CHART

Name of Part	Quantity	Diameter (inches)	Length (inches)	Description
Planter - part A	23	¾	10	straight
Trellis - part B	7	¼–½	24	pliable
Trellis brace	1	¼–½	20	pliable

DIRECTIONS

Cutting the Branches
1. Cut 23 twigs, ¾" in diameter, for the main planter parts A, each 10" long.
2. Cut 7 pliable twigs, ¼" to ½" in diameter, for the trellis parts B, each 24" long.
3. Cut 1 pliable twig, ¼" to ½" in diameter, for the trellis brace C, 20" long.

Drilling the Branches
1. With a pencil, mark one inch from both ends of all twigs A.
2. Drill a pilot hole large enough to accommodate your finishing nails through each of the 46 pencil marks.

Building the Bottom
1. Arrange two twigs A, approximately 10" apart and parallel on the work table. Lay one side twig A at a right angle across the

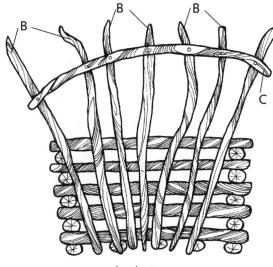

#1   back view

two parallel twigs, making sure that the pre-drilled pilot holes line up. NOTE: All right angle parts extend approximately 1". Nail in place.

2. Repeat with opposite end.

3. Approximately 2" from each attached twig, center three twigs A across the parallel twigs. Nail in place.

Building the Planter

1. The planter is built by alternating parts A in a log-building manner. Remaining construction is nailed in place at an angle to prevent nails from hitting nails. Side parts should parallel the bottom.

2. Begin by laying a twig across the four bottom side twigs. Nail in place, at an angle, using thin finishing nails.

3. Repeat on opposite side and nail in place.

4. Repeat the above procedure until all A parts are used.

Adding the Trellis

1. Begin adding the trellis twigs from the center. Using pilot hole and nail construction attach the center trellis twig to the bottom and top planter parts.

2. Add the neighboring trellis twigs, the top ends gently fanned out using the same method as above.

3. Repeat with the remaining four trellis twigs B.

4. Gently bend trellis brace C. Place C across the seven standing trellis twigs approximately 8" from the top. Drill and nail in place where C meets the seven B parts.

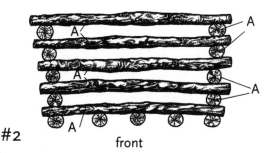

#2   front

Plant Pedestal

"I got a large round of thick green moss, and some strawberry-vines mingled with it, and a delicate little fern to plant right in the center ... "

MRS. JULIA MCNAIR WRIGHT, 1883

THIS NATURAL PLANT STAND, TALL AND STATELY, can make any corner feel like a country garden, whether it's the winter parlor, or summer porch. The center shelf guarantees stability, while serving as the perfect perch for trailing plants. Try some unusual ivy varieties such as gnome, spetchley, or Irish lace.

MATERIALS   *Skill Level: experienced*
Any pliable hardwood (such as willow, beech, birch, cherry, or hickory) may be used. The branches need to be flexible to permit slight bending during construction. You will need eight 46"

lengths, ¾" in diameter; four 8 ½" lengths, ½" in diameter; and two 1 ¾" thick pieces of scrap wood.

TOOLS

- Single bit axe for felling trees
- Crosscut hand saw
- Clippers or garden shears
- Ruler or measuring tape
- Marking pencil
- Drill with a selection of bits
- Hammer
- Safety goggles
- Work gloves

CUTTING CHART

Name of Part	Quantity	Diameter (inches)	Length (inches)	Description
Legs A	4	¾	46	hardwood/pliable
Legs A1	4	¾	46	hardwood/pliable
Platform B	1	1 ¾ thick	8 × 8 square	lumber/pliable
Center platform C	1	1 ¾ thick	6 × 6 square	lumber/pliable
Braces D	4	½	8 ½	hardwood/pliable

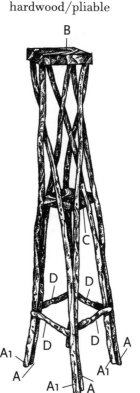

Cutting the Branches

1. Cut eight ¾" diameter branches for legs A and A1, each 46" long.
2. Cut four ½" diameter branches for the braces D, each 8 ½" long.

DIRECTIONS

Laying Out the Sub-Assembly

1. Place the platform B on the workbench. Refer to diagram 4 placement of legs A, and mark the location for the four legs.
2. With pilot hole and nail construction, add one leg to the underside of the platform.

#1

center platform C

#2

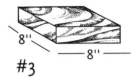

#3

3. Nail the attached leg to a corner of the center platform as shown in diagram 6.
4. Repeat leg-to-platform-to-center platform installation with the three remaining legs A.

Attaching Legs A1

1. Refer to diagram 5. Using a pencil, mark A1 locations. With pilot hole and nail construction, attach one leg A1 in place.
2. Carefully bend leg A1 and attach to the center platform at a slant, under the corner leg A. (Refer to diagram 7.)
3. Repeat steps 1 and 2 above with the remaining three legs A1.

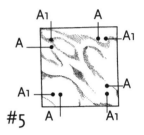

#5

Adding the Braces

1. Mark a location 8" from the bottom of legs A.
2. Butt one brace D between two legs A at the 8" mark. Nail in place with pilot hole and nail construction. NOTE: The braces are butted between the A legs, and are outside the A1 legs.
3. Continue to butt, drill, and nail the remaining three braces in place, as in step 2.
4. Make sure your plant pedestal stands straight. Trim the legs, if needed.

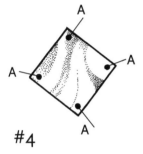

A

A

A

A

#4

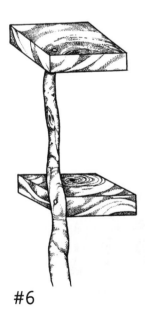

#6

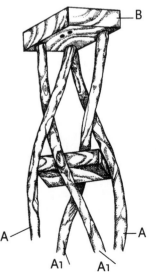

#7

CHAPTER 5

Bird Houses & Feeders

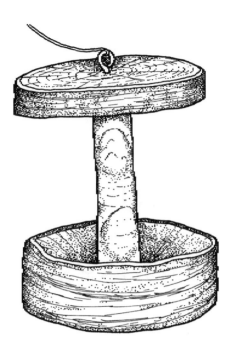

Basic Bird Feeder

"I come from fields once tall with wheat,
from pastures deep in fern and thistle;
I come from vales of meadowsweet,
and I love to whistle."   E.B. WHITE

BIRD FEEDERS COME IN A SURPRISING ARRAY OF SHAPES AND sizes. Nature enthusiasts and, more importantly, birds seem especially fond of this model. Easy enough to make in a day, you may want several to hang around your property or to give as gifts. Be sure to search the firewood pile for nicely marked logs and branches. Suspended from a tree limb or mounted on a post, this feeder blends gracefully with nature.

MATERIALS   *Skill Level: intermediate +*

Choose two 6" diameter white birch slices, 1" thick for the top, and 2" thick for the bottom. NOTE: Any hardwood such as hickory, maple, or beech may be used. You will also need one 1 ½" diameter branch, 6" long for the center post. Four 1 ½" galvanized roofing nails and a screw-eye for hanging are also neccessary.

TOOLS
- Single bit axe for felling trees, if you don't have a wood pile
- Crosscut hand saw
- Sandpaper (optional)
- Ruler or measuring tape
- Marking pencil
- Woodcarver's gouge and mallet
- Drill and a selection of bits
- Hammer
- Clippers or garden shears
- Safety goggles
- Heavy duty work gloves

DIRECTIONS Begin by sanding on both sides of the top wood slice and only one side of the bottom slice.

Shaping the Feeder

NOTE: The gouge is a potentially dangerous hand tool. Wear heavy duty work gloves and safety glasses to avoid cuts and flying wood chips.

1. With a dark pencil, mark a ½" margin around the circumference of the bottom wood slice.
2. Use the woodcarver's gouge and mallet to begin chipping a depression across the middle. Turn the wood slice as you work and continue to chip at an angle from opposite sides. Aim for a shallow angle along the rim with a concave bottom.
3. When the bottom has reached a depth of 1½", add the 6" long center post.

Assembling the Feeder

1. Center the 6" long post on the underside of the 1" thick top slice. Using pilot hole and nail construction with two nails, join the top piece to the post from the outside.
2. Position the 6" long center post in the base of the gouged out bottom. Attach the two pieces from the bottom, using two nails and pilot hole construction to avoid splitting the wood. Center and join the 1" thick remaining slice to the center post from the top.
3. Add a galvanized metal screw-eye and rope for hanging, or mount on a post.

Bark
Teepee
Bird
House

*"Make a place safe for birds and the birds
will find it out and occupy it."*

C.C. ABBOT

TEST YOUR BARK PEELING SKILLS WITH THIS CHARMING
7" tall teepee, perfect for chickadees and house wrens. The 1 ⅛"
diameter opening and lack of perch help to reduce the chances
of sparrows using the hole or bothering the chicks. This classic
North American design lends itself to indoor display, and can be
made in a variety of sizes to grace shelves and window ledges.

MATERIALS

Skill Level: beginner

You will need one sheet of peeled bark for the teepee, 8" wide and 12" long, and one sheet of peeled bark for the teepee floor, approximately 8" × 8". You will also need a ¼" diameter supple willow shoot, 24" long for forming the bottom rim; a 6" long straight branch and twine or rawhide for hanging; and peeled bark strips for lacing, ⅛" wide. Two pattern pieces, teepee pattern, and teepee floor pattern, are provided. NOTE: To prepare the patterns, enlarge on a photocopier at percentage given.

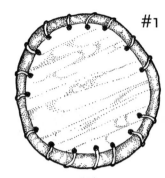

#1

laced bottom

TOOLS

- Clippers or garden shears
- Ruler or measuring tape
- Marking pencil
- Scissors
- Leather hole punch or awl
- Large-eye needle and heavy thread

DIRECTIONS

Assembling the Teepee

1. Enlarge the teepee pattern by 133% on a photocopier, and use to trace the pattern onto the back of the bark. Cut out the teepee using the scissors, and gently form into the cone-shape. NOTE: The ends overlap to form the teepee.

2. Using the hole punch (or awl) punch holes evenly, approximately ½" apart along the overlapping ends, as shown in the diagram. Using the peeled bark strip, lace the teepee together through the punched holes. For increased strength, lace all parts together with the needle and heavy thread first, and then add the peeled bark.

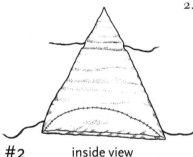

#2   inside view

3. Using the awl, cut out a 1 ⅛" diameter opening on the front of the teepee.

4. Copy teepee floor. Mark around the pattern onto the

back of the 8" × 8" piece of bark with a marking pencil. Cut out the teepee floor using the scissors. Adjust the circumference, if necessary. Using the awl (or hole punch) punch holes evenly, approximately ½" to ¾" apart along the outside edge.

5. Carefully bend a 24" long pliable willow shoot (or other supple branch) into a ring and fit it along the edge of the teepee floor. Using the peeled bark strip (or needle and heavy thread first) lace the willow shoot in place along the outside edge of the floor as in step 2 above.

6. Lace the floor to the teepee using the peeled bark strip.

Adding the Hanger

#3

1. Punch holes from the outside of the teepee on both sides approximately 1 ½" to 2" from the top. Place a straight ¼" diameter branch through the holes inside the teepee. Attach twine or rawhide, knotted and tied, as shown in the drawing.

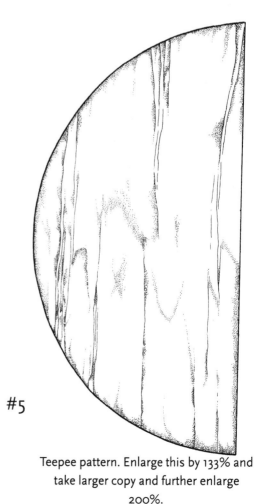

#5

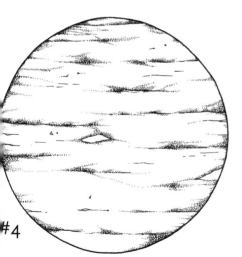

#4

Teepee floor pattern. Enlarge the pattern by 133% and take that copy and enlarge by 200%.

Teepee pattern. Enlarge this by 133% and take larger copy and further enlarge 200%.

Willow Log Cabin Bird House

"I hear the birds make music fit for angels ... "
ISLE OF INNISFREE, IRISH BALLAD

CRAFTED FROM SCRAP WOOD AND WILLOW TWIGS, THE galvanized tin roof helps to protect the birds in stormy weather and makes the structure easy to hang from any tree limb. The drawer is an idea borrowed from bird cages, and is a functional element for cleaning out the house after the tenants have moved. You will need moderate carpentry skills to construct the basic cabin. If you're dubious about building it yourself, have someone skilled help you, or try nailing willow twigs on a purchased bird house.

MATERIALS
Skill Level: experienced
House size, approximately 5" × 5" × 8 ½" high.
    1 piece ½" pine board 6" × 36" long, or an assortment of scrap

The Gothic Arm Chair

So sturdy and natural that it could grow right from the ground, the Gothic Arm Chair combines all the best qualities of rustic furniture.

The Garden Gate
Keeping intruders out, or beauty in, the fanciful Garden Gate is at home anywhere. Lean it up against an old wall or place it at the entrance to your garden.

The Garden Chair
This simple, elegant chair is perfect place for the weary gardener to sit, surveying the green and flowered kingdom all round.

*The Birch and Copper Feeder &
The Willow Log Cabin*
The Birch and Copper Feeder is an attractive way to draw birds to your garden.

*The Robin's Nesting House and
The Willow Log Cabin Bird House*
Invite the harbinger of spring to become a long term guest with this simple nesting house. The Willow Log Cabin shows the drawer for easy cleaning.

*The Willow Log
Cabin Bird House*
Visiting birds will appreciate this whimsical version of a rustic log cabin.

The Scarecrow
The Scarecrow will keep out the birds and add a touch of rustic whimsey to your garden.

The Wattle Border Fence
This lovely little fence is just the thing to hem in your low growing plants and shrubs, and line your rocky garden paths.

The Cedar and Vine Garden Bench
The Cedar and Vine Garden Bench is a rustic showpiece for the garden or porch.

The Sundial
The Sundial is a charming addition to any garden. The sundial top can be purchased at most garden centers.

The Twig Hanger
Hang your herbs and
favorite flowers to dry on
this handy twig hanger.

Scallop Edging
Scallop edging turns a simple fence into a timeless garden classic.

The Willy Loveseat
The Willy is a timeless design that will grace your garden for many years. Add a pillow or two to make it even more comfortable.

The Summer House
The Summer House will be a peaceful place of lasting beauty. A true
rustic classic.

wood for the basic house and drawer, along with carpenter's wood glue. You will also need an assortment of twigs with diameters of ¼" to ¾", and 7" long. Galvanized, corrugated tin 8" × 12" is required for the roof, along with #4 aluminum cut tacks, ½" finishing nails and one galvanized screw-eye hook for hanging. Seven pattern pieces for the front, back, sides, bottom, and drawer are provided. Photocopy them and use them to trace out the patterns.

TOOLS
- Crosscut hand saw
- Keyhole saw
- Table saw or power saw (optional)
  NOTE: These are potentially dangerous tools and should be used only by an experienced operator who knows how to use them safely.
- Shears or clippers
- Ruler or measuring tape
- Marking pencil
- Hammer
- Safety goggles
- Work gloves

DIRECTIONS

Cutting the Cabin

1. Photocopy all pattern pieces and cut out. Using a pencil, trace all cabin pattern pieces on the ½" pine.
2. Using the saw, cut out one cabin bottom.
3. Cut out two cabin ends; on each piece, bevel one short edge at a 45-degree angle.
4. Cut out one cabin front; cut the entrance hole, using the keyhole saw.
5. Cut out one cabin back.

#1

Cutting the Drawer

1. Using a pencil, trace all drawer pattern pieces on the ½" pine.
2. Using the saw, cut one drawer bottom.
3. Cut out two drawer sides.
4. Cut out one drawer front.
5. Cut out one drawer back.

Building the Cabin

1. Apply glue to the side edges of one cabin end piece. With the beveled edge up, stand up the front and back pieces on a workbench parallel to each other and place one cabin end between them, so that the edges are square.
2. Use finishing nails hammered at each corner to guarantee a tight fit.
3. Repeat the above 2 steps with the remaining cabin end.
4. Apply a ½" bead of glue on the cabin bottom. Place it on the workbench.
5. Place the cabin construction on the glued bottom, making sure the edges are flush and square.
6. Repeat step 2 above.

#2

Building the Drawer

1. Apply glue to the back edge of the drawer bottom piece. Place the drawer back against it, making sure the edge is flush and square. Use two finishing nails to secure.
2. Apply glue along a back edge and bottom edge. Place one drawer side piece against the glued edges so that the bottom and side edges are flush. Use finishing nails to secure the side piece to the back and to the bottom.
3. Repeat with the remaining side piece.

#3

4. Apply glue to both ends of the side pieces, and the bottom edge. Place the drawer front, with the wider side up, against the drawer side edges flush and square with the bottom. Secure to bottom and sides with finishing nails. NOTE: The drawer front extends outside the cabin opening to permit for easy removal.

#4

Adding the "Logs"

1. Using the ruler and pencil, measure and mark 14 ¾" diameter twigs to outline the cabin edges. To prevent splitting, use the pilot hole and nail technique. Attach the twigs to all outside edges with thin finishing nails.

#5

2. Using the garden shears, cut and nail the ¼" to ¾" diameter twigs as you proceed so they face the cabin. Place a forked twig just under the entrance hole for a perch.

3. Arrange a supple twig in a "U" shape to form the drawer pull, and install along placement dots as indicated on the drawer front pattern.

Adding the Tin Roof

1. Fold the 8" × 12" galvanized tin in half to form the peaked roof. The roof overhangs the house approximately 2" along the sides and 1 ½" over the front and back of the cabin. Arrange the roof over the house along the beveled edges, and drill holes for the aluminum cut tacks at the locations where the roof meets the edges of the house. Drill a hole along the top ridge for the galvanized screw-eye.

#6

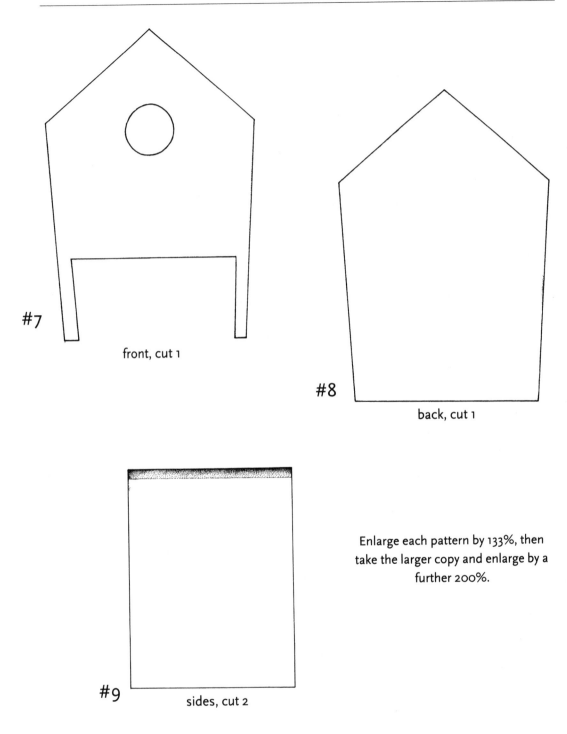

#7

front, cut 1

#8

back, cut 1

#9   sides, cut 2

Enlarge each pattern by 133%, then
take the larger copy and enlarge by a
further 200%.

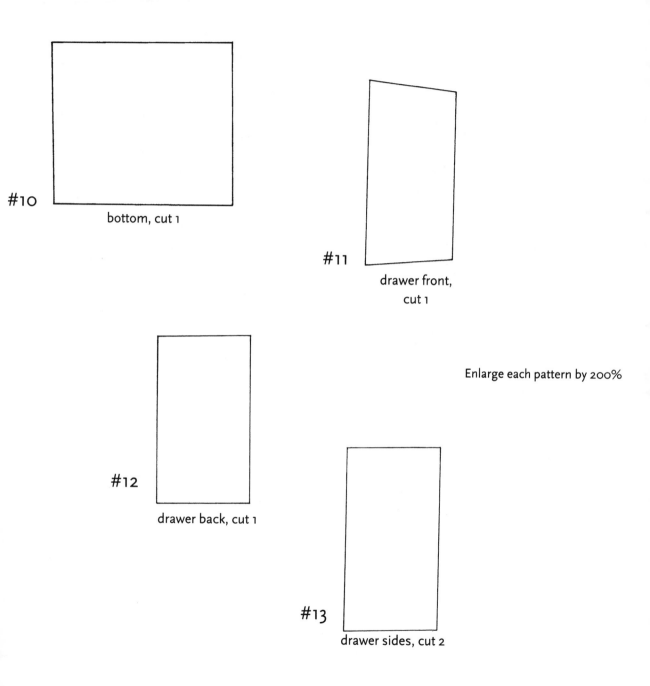

#10

bottom, cut 1

#11

drawer front,
cut 1

Enlarge each pattern by 200%

#12

drawer back, cut 1

#13

drawer sides, cut 2

Laced Bark Bird House

INTERIOR DESIGN THEMES INCREASINGLY BRING THE outdoors inside with a host of decorative items, and bird houses displayed as small works of art top the list of favorite rustic items. With its peeled bark, this charming model creates the illusion of a miniature woodland indoors, whether it's placed on the coffee table or used as a centerpiece for a special dinner. If you choose to hang it outdoors, you will provide shelter for nest-building families of wrens or chickadees, nuthatches or titmouses.

MATERIALS   *Skill Level: intermediate*

You will need one 4" × 4" pine board ½" thick for the base and a selection of bark sheets, four 8" wide and 10" long for the sides, and four 10" wide and 7" long for the roof. You will also need a selection of straight branches such as willow, hickory or maple, 5" to 10" long and ¾" in diameter to construct the birdhouse. Bark or vine strips are required for lacing (heavy thread and a large-eye needle are optional for extra strength). Four galvanized roofing nails are used to attach the roof, ¾" carpet tacks to attach the bark to the base, and one metal screw-eye, washer, and nut are used for hanging the birdhouse. You will also need heavy books or bricks for pressing the bark flat. Patterns are provided for the birdhouse sides and roof. To prepare the patterns, enlarge on a photocopy machine at the percentage given.

TOOLS
- Clippers or garden shears
- Ruler or measuring tape
- Marking pencil
- Scissors and sharp pocket knife
- Leather hole punch or awl
- Tack hammer
- Large-eye needle and heavy thread (optional)
- Work gloves

#1

DIRECTIONS   *Cutting the Bark Sheets*

1. Place the flattened bark pieces, face down, on the work table. Using the enlarged pattern, trace the outline of the bird house side on the back of the bark. Using the scissors cut out one house side.
2. Repeat step 1 on the three remaining bird house sides.
3. Choose one side for the front. Using the scissors or a sharp knife, cut out a 1 ¼" diameter entrance hole, and small perch hole as the side pattern indicates.
4. Place the flattened bark pieces, face down, on the work table. Using the pattern, trace the outline of the bird house roof on

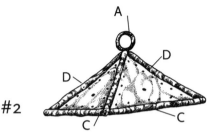

#2

the back of the bark. Cut out one house roof.

5.   Repeat step 3 with the three remaining bird house roof parts.

Cutting the Branches

NOTE: You will need pliable branches for the slight bending that is required to shape the house.

1. Cut four ¾" diameter straight branches, each 10" long for the side rails A.
2. Cut four ¾" diameter straight branches, each 8" long for the tie beams B.
3. Cut four ¾" diameter straight branches, each 10" long for the ridge beams C.
4. Cut four ¾" diameter straight branches, each 8" long for the ridge poles D.

Framing the House

1. Place the 4" × 4" base on the work table. With the pencil, mark a point at each corner for the ¾" side rails A. With pilot hole and nail construction attach each side rail to the base, from the bottom.
2. Stand the base (with attached side rails) up. Butt one tie beam B, between two side rails A, at the top. Check for a tight fit; use the garden shears to make any necessary adjustments. Using pilot hole and nail construction, join B to both side rails.
3. Repeat step 2 with the remaining tie beams B.

Adding the Sides

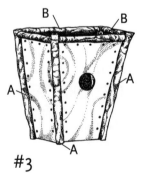

#3

1. Select one bark side, and place it under two side rails A, and under the tie beam B, with its bottom end flush against the base, making sure it fits properly, and trimming if need be.
2. Using the hole punch (or awl), make holes along the top and both sides, approximately ½" in and 2" apart.

3. Using the ¾" carpet tacks, tack the bottom edge of one bark side to the wooden base at evenly spaced intervals.
4. Repeat step 3 with the remaining bark sheets.
5. Join the bark to the framework using split bark or vine, by lacing through the holes diagonally over the branch and through the bark.

NOTE: For increased strength, you may choose to lace all the parts together with the needle and heavy thread first, and then add the bark or vine for embellishment.

Making and Adding the Roof

1. Using the hole punch (or awl) punch holes evenly at approximately ½" in, and 1" apart along all four sides of each bark roof section.
2. Arrange and adjust each roof part behind the ridge beams C, and the ridge poles D. Following the directions in step 5 above, lace the sections together.
3. Attach the metal screw-eye to the roof peak with the connecting washer and nut inside the roof.
4. Rest the completed roof structure on top of the house. Mark the four points where the roofing nails will be added. Using the drill and bit, drill pilot holes at these points to join the roof to the tie beams B. Remember to use a drill bit one size smaller than your nail to guarantee a snug fit.

Enlarge both patterns by 200%, then take the larger patterns and enlarge them by a further 200%.

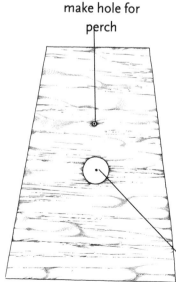

make hole for perch

#5

1¼" diameter hole

sides, cut 4

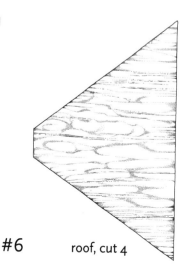

#6　　　roof, cut 4

Thatched Roof Bird House

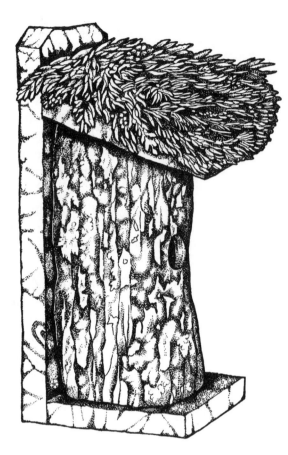

"Hi! My little hut
is newly-thatched
I see Blue Morning
Glories."

ISSA (1763–1827)

THE COZY THATCHED-ROOF COTTAGES FOUND NESTLED IN Irish glens are the inspiration for this lift-top, hollow-log model. The hinged top helps to make cleaning easy after each brood has fledged, and the backboard makes it simple to mount along a picket garden fence. Any dry grass can be used for the thatching. This particular roof is made of dried winter fern fronds.

MATERIALS   *Skill Level: intermediate*
Use a 4" diameter log 9" long for the house. One piece of 1" lumber, 5 ½" wide and 25" long is required for the construction.

Seven galvanized nails, two small butterfly hinges, and finishing nails are needed to assemble the structure. Narrow gauge wire (or string) will be required for thatching the roof.

TOOLS
- Single bit axe for felling trees
- Coping saw
- Crosscut hand saw
- Ruler or measuring tape
- Marking pencil
- Carpenter's gouge or woodcarving chisel
- Mallet
- Brace and bit (optional)
- Drill with a selection of bits, including woodboring bit
- Safety goggles
- Work gloves

NOTE: The log requires a 2 ½" cavity for the nesting compartment. One method is to use a power drill and make several large holes in a circular pattern, then further shape the opening with a chisel and mallet. A brace and bit work just as well but take longer. Choose a steel-shanked ratchet brace with a 10" sweep, and an expansive bit that makes a hole 2" across. This method may still require a chisel and mallet to make the cavity slightly larger.

#1

DIRECTIONS
1. Stand the 4" diameter, 9" long log on the work table. Draw a 2 ½" diameter circle on the bottom of the log.
2. Using one of the methods mentioned above, bore a 2 ½" diameter hole lengthwise completely through the log.
3. Center a pencil mark 2" down from

#2

the top of the log. Using the drill and woodboring bit, create a 1" opening through the log for the entrance hole.

4. Place the 5 ½" × 25" piece of 1" lumber on the workbench. Cut one piece 13" long for the backboard A; one piece 6" long for the base B; and one piece 6" long for the roof C.

5. Butt base B against backboard A. Using two nails and pilot hole construction, nail backboard to base from the back.

6. Place the hollow 9" tall log on the workbench. It is necessary to cut the top of the log at a slant, making the front of the house 1" shorter than the back. Make a mark 8" from the bottom on the front of the house. Using a hand saw, cut the log at a slant, from the top of the 9" back to the 8" front mark. This permits the roof to be attached at an angle.

7. Center the hollow log house on the base B with the entrance hole facing out. Using pilot hole construction, attach the log house to the base from the bottom of the base using galvanized nails.

8. Rest the roof section along the top of the log and adjust the log top if necessary. Install the butterfly hinge along the roof section C, and the adjacent backboard A. Test to make sure it flips open properly.

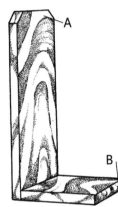

#3

The house is now tenant-worthy.

Thatching the Roof

Covering the roof is fun and adds a different dimension to the structure. Learning to thatch a small area is easy, and the technique can be applied to various other projects. Any dry grass, straw, hay, rye, oats, dry weed, or wildflower may be used for thatching. Fern fronds are gathered during late autumn or winter, when their naturally dry brown stalks are easy to locate in

#4

patches along streams and creek beds. To dry ripe green grasses, gather them in the spring or summer. Hang them in bunches, or spread them to dry in a cool place. For a bleached effect, dry them in full sun. To prevent mildew, store any dried material in a cool, airy location, free of moisture.

Thatching consists of gathering small bundles together, wrapping and binding, and tying additional bundles together.

Begin with step 1: Gather six thatch pieces together; wrap and bind with wire (or string); add two more bundles as shown in step 2. Attach the three-bundle collection to the roof at the front edge, using wire staples or finishing nails. Create two groups of six bundles, as shown in step 3, with the wrap and bind method. Attach to the roof, over the installed bundles, trimmed 1" to 2" shorter, with wire staples or finishing nails. Add step 4 as before. Continue to add bundles until the area is covered and you are satisfied with the arrangement.

step 1

#5

step 2

#6

step 3

#7

#8

step 4

The Finch House

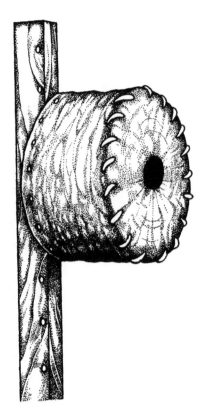

"The goldfinch on a thistle-head
Stood scattering seedlets as she fed ... "
J. INGELOW

CHECK THE FOREST FLOOR FOR SHEETS OF NATURALLY PEELED
bark for this design. The house finch requires a 7" deep nesting
compartment, but a smaller bird like a chickadee should have a
compartment 4" deep. By using this same basic design and altering the depth, you will be able to make a variety of houses. To attract house finches, mount the house eight to twelve feet above
the ground.

MATERIALS   *Skill Level: intermediate*
You will need one oval wood back, 6" × 10" and ½" thick. A selection of bark sheets; the house sheet is 7" × 29" , and the front is 7"
× 10 ½". Locating exact size sheets is ideal; smaller sheets may be

pieced together, however, and will work just as well. You will also need a selection of willow shoots or other pliable branches 33" to 40" long and ⅛" to ¼" in diameter for the inside rim. Bark or vine strips are required for lacing, and ¾" carpet tacks are used to attach the bark to the oval wood back. A dab of glue may be needed to join the bark sheets if you are piecing the sheets.

TOOLS
- Clippers or garden shears
- Ruler or measuring tape
- Marking pencil
- Scissors
- Sharp pocket knife (optional)
- Leather hole punch or awl
- Tack hammer
- Heavy thread and large-eye needle
- Spring-type clothespins for temporary holding
- Work gloves

DIRECTIONS

Cutting the Bark Sheets

1. Place the flattened bark pieces on the work table. Using the scissors and cutting with the grain, cut a 7" wide bark sheet 29" long, or cut enough pieces to obtain the correct measurement to surround the outside rim of the 6" × 10" oval wood bottom.
2. Cut one oval bark piece approximately 7" × 10 ½" for the bird house front.

Building the Bird House

1. Center one, or more bark sheets along the outside rim of the 6" × 10" oval wooden bottom. Using carpet tacks, fasten the bark to the base at evenly spaced intervals.
2. If more than one sheet is needed, overlap the bark sheets and seal the edges with glue. Continue to tack the sheets to the bottom, at evenly spaced intervals, until the bottom is enfolded.

Adding the Top Rim

1. Using the hole punch (or awl), make holes along the top rim of the bark sheet ½" in from the top and approximately 2" apart.
2. Gently bend one pliable willow shoot into an oval and fit it carefully inside the bark rim. Clamp the willow shoot to the bark with clothespins to hold it in place until the sewing is completed.
3. Join the oval willow shoot to the bark rim using heavy thread and a needle, by sewing through the holes diagonally over the willow shoot and through the bark. Knot the end to secure, and remove the clothespins.

Adding the House Front

1. Cut one bark sheet for the front into an oval approximately 7" × 10 ½", adjusting it to fit along the outside circumference of the house.
2. Mark a center point on the bark oval; using the scissors (or sharp knife) cut a hole with a 1 ½" diameter for the entrance.
3. Join the house front to the house using split bark or vine, by lacing through the hole diagonally, as in step 3 above. If split bark is unavailable, use heavy-duty thread as before.

Place the entrance hole away from the prevailing winds, and attach it to a post 8 to 12 feet above the ground.

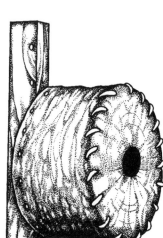

attach back board to fence post or yardstake
8–12 feet above the ground

#1

Robin's Nesting House

"Little Bob Robin,
Where do you live?
Up in yonder wood, sir,
On a hazel twig."   NURSERY RHYME

THIS NESTING ROOST IS PERFECT FOR THE GARDEN AREA AND probably will attract other roosting birds, such as swallows, phoebes, and mourning doves. The first signs of spring make us think of turning the soil, sowing seeds, digging in the dirt and, of course, the robin redbreast. Put up one of these houses, and leave it up all year, and you can welcome the robin back every spring as harbinger of a new growing season.

MATERIALS   *Skill Level: beginner*
Use any hardwood wood slabs such as cedar or maple for the nesting house which measures 8" wide, 11" high, and 7" deep. Its

roof is constructed of two wood slabs, each 10" × 11". The exaggerated overhang provides additional protection. One ¾" diameter ridge pole, 12" long is required; and one 1" diameter branch, 11" long for the front brace. Wood slabs, cut from firewood work up very nicely for this project. The 8" × 9" floor is constructed of ½" pine. Galvanized flat head (and roofing) nails are used for the joinery.

TOOLS
- Single bit axe for felling trees
- Crosscut hand saw
- Saber saw (optional)
- Ruler or measuring tape
- Marking pencil
- Hammer and nails
- Drill with a selection of bits
- Safety goggles
- Work gloves

CUTTING CHART

Name of part	Quantity	Diameter (inches)	Length (inches)	Description
Floor A	1	8 - wide	9 ½	½" pine
Sides B	2	6 - wide	8	1 ½" thick slab wood
Back C	1	11 - wide	11	1 ½" thick slab wood
Ridge pole D	1	¾	12	straight
Roof E	2	10 - wide	11	1 ½" thick slab wood
Front brace F	1	1	11	straight and split

DIRECTIONS

Cutting the Parts

1. Cut the 8" × 9 ½" floor A, out of ½" pine.
2. Cut two sides B, each 6" wide and 8" high, out of 1 ½" thick slab wood.
3. Mark a center line

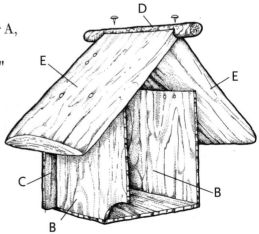

#1

on the 11" × 11" wood back C. Make a mark along both outside edges at approximately 5" down from the top. Cut the peaked shape from the top of the center line, at a slant, down to the five-inch mark, thereby forming the peak for the back, C.

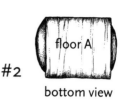

#2

bottom view

4. Cut one ¾" diameter branch for the ridge pole D, 12" long.
5. Cut two roof parts E, each 10" wide and 11" long, out of 1 ½" thick slab wood.
6. Cut one 1" diameter branch for the front brace F, 11" long. Cut this branch in half lengthwise.

Assembling the House

1. With the bark side out, arrange one side part along the outside edge of the 8" × 9" pine floor, allowing approximately 1" to overhang the floor. Drill pilot holes from the bottom of the floor and approximately ¾" through the side part. Secure with galvanized flathead nails.
2. Repeat with the remaining side part.
3. With the bark side out, arrange the back in place. NOTE: At this point, it is likely that the floor extends beyond the back part. Using pilot hole and nail construction attach the back part to the floor.
4. With the bark side out, nail the split 11" long front brace F, along the bottom floor edge with pilot hole and nail construction and galvanized nails.

Adding the Roof

1. Referring to diagram 5, slant one of the roof pieces E over the back with the

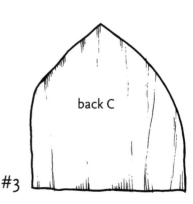

back C

#3

bark side out, allowing the roof to overlap the back approximately 1". Drill two holes through the roof into the back, and nail in place. Drill two holes through the roof into the side B, and nail in place.

2. Repeat to attach the second roof part.
3. Place the ¾" ridgepole in the space between the two roof parts. Drill a hole, at each end, through the ridgepole into the roof parts and nail in place.

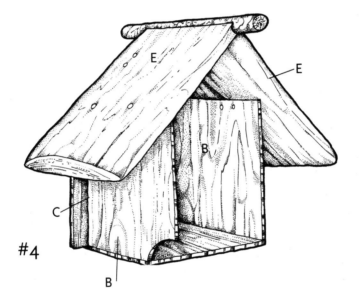

Birch & Copper Feeder

THE TOP LIFTS OFF THIS WHITE BIRCH FEEDER TO ALLOW FOR easy refilling, while the copper plates surrounding the openings prevent unwanted visitors like squirrels from entering. This design with its four openings invites several guests to dine at the same time.

MATERIALS   *Skill Level: intermediate*
Use a white birch log, 9" to 10" long and 4" to 5" in diameter, or other hardwoods such as beech, hickory, or cedar for the feeder.

135

You will need two 6" to 7" diameter wood slices, 3" thick for the base and roof. A sheet of copper, 6" × 24" will be required, along with twenty 1" Phillips-head screws, and two U-shaped (or screw-eye) hangers. Four ⅛" diameter twigs, 3" long are used for perches, and twine or rawhide for hanging.

TOOLS
- Single bit axe for felling trees, if you don't have a wood pile
- Crosscut hand saw
- Brace and bit
- Sandpaper
- Ruler or measuring tape
- Marking pencil
- Drill and a selection of bits, including a woodboring bit and expansive bit
- Tin snips
- Carpenter's compass
- Phillips-head screwdriver
- Safety goggles
- Work gloves

DIRECTIONS   *Building the Feeder*

1. The feeder requires a 3" to 4" cavity for the feeding compartment. With luck, a wood pile, or walk in the woods will offer a partially hollow log. If you have to bore out the center of the log, stand the 9" to 10" long, 4" to 5" diameter log on the workbench. Draw a 3" to 4" diameter circle on the top of the log. Using the power drill, or brace and bit, bore a 3" to 4" diameter hole completely through the log.

2. Center a pencil mark approximately

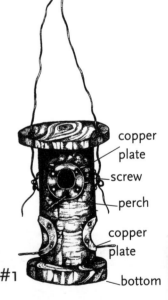

copper plate

screw

perch

copper plate

#1   bottom

#2

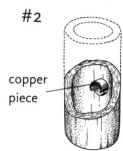

copper
piece

inside view showing copper
opening cover (NOTE:
these are placed over every
opening)

2 ½" down from the top of the log on the front and on the
back of the log. Using the drill and woodboring bit, create a
1" opening on the front side and on the back side.

3. Center a pencil mark 2 ½" up from the bottom of the log on
   the front and on the back of the log. Using the drill and
   woodboring bit, create a 1"
   opening as above.

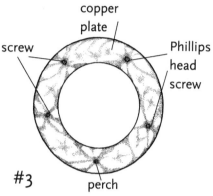

copper
plate

screw

Phillips
head
screw

#3

perch

Adding Copper Plates and Shields

1. Using a carpenter's
   compass, cut out four
   copper plates 3" to 3 ½" in
   diameter. Arrange a
   copper plate over a 1"
   opening. Using the
   compass, center a 1" circle
   on the copper plate, and
   using the tin snips cut out the opening. Repeat with the
   remaining three copper plates.

2. Arrange a plate over the 1" opening. Using the drill and bit,
   drill five holes through the plate and the log, as shown in the
   copper plate diagram 3. Attach plate to log with four
   Phillips-head screws, leaving the bottom hole unattached for
   the twig perch.

3. Repeat with the remaining three
   copper plates.

4. Cut four pieces of sheet copper approximately 2" × 2". Bend slightly, and fit
   along the upper section of each 1"
   opening, as illustrated in diagram 2.

Final Assembly

1. Place the feeder on the workbench,
   bottom side up. Center one 6" to 7"

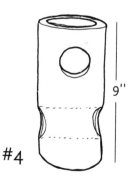

9"

#4

diameter log slice, 3" thick (the bottom) on the feeder bottom. Using pilot hole and nail construction, join the bottom to the feeder with two galvanized nails.

2. Arrange U-shaped hanging hooks along the sides of the feeder, approximately 3" down from the top. Attach with Phillips-head screws.

3. Drill two holes through the log slice top. Place the top on the feeder, and hold in place by threading twine through the U-shaped hangers and the drilled holes.

To fill, lift off the top and pour in bird seed. Hang outdoors from a tree limb or post.

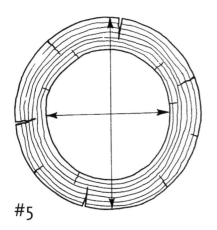

#5

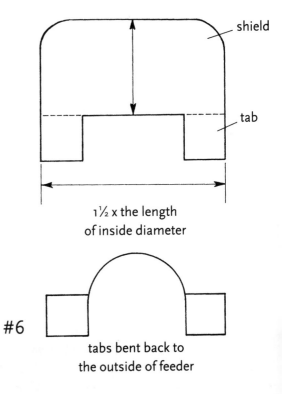

shield

tab

1½ x the length
of inside diameter

#6

tabs bent back to
the outside of feeder

Grapevine Roof Feeder

I value my garden more for being full of blackbirds than of cherries, and very frankly give them fruit for their song.
JOSEPH ADDISON

AN AFTERNOON IS ALL IT WILL TAKE TO CRAFT THIS BIRD feeder. Gathering materials is simple because any kind of twigs will do. This easy-to-make feeder is great fun to build, and very rewarding when you observe the birds feeding at the generously sized tray. Hang from a tree with rope.

MATERIALS **Skill Level: beginner**
You will need a selection of 1" diameter hardwood twigs, including two forked twigs, ranging in length from 8" to 12". An 8 ½" × 12" piece of scrap lumber, ½" thick is required for the tray.

Gather enough vines to weave the top (any local vine, such as grapevine, Virginia creeper, bittersweet, wisteria, or kudzu). Galvanized 1 ½" metal roofing nails, 1" finishing nails, and a length of rope 20" long for hanging are also needed.

TOOLS
- Single bit axe for felling trees
- Crosscut hand saw
- Ruler or measuring tape
- Marking pencil
- Clippers or garden shears
- Drill and a selection of bits
- Hammer and galvanized nails
- Safety goggles
- Work gloves

CUTTING CHART

Name of Part	Quantity	Diameter (inches)	Length (inches)	Description
Tray ends A	2	1	8 ½	straight
Tray sides B	2	1	12	straight
Roof supports C	4	1	8	straight
Roof peak braces D	2	1	16–20	*forked
Roof side brace E	2	1	11	straight
Ridge pole F	1	1	11	straight

*Forks form the peaks, therefore select branches that can be trimmed at both ends of the fork. The ridge pole will be installed, at the forks, between the two roof peak braces D.

DIRECTIONS

Cutting the Branches

1. Cut two 1" diameter branches, 8 ½" long for the tray ends A.
2. Cut two 1" diameter branches, 12" long for the tray sides B.
3. Cut four 1" diameter branches, 8" long for the roof supports C.
4. Cut two forked 1" diameter branches, 16" to 20" long for the roof peak braces D.

5. Cut two 1" diameter branches, 11" long for the roof side braces E.
6. Cut one straight 1" diameter branch, 11" long for the ridge pole F.
7. Cut a piece of ½" pine, 8 ½" × 12" for the feeder tray.
8. Approximately 25 pieces of supple vines, 15" to 20" long are required for weaving the roof.

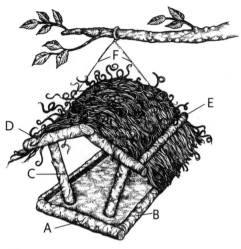

#1

Drilling the Pilot Holes and Assembling the Tray

Make the pilot hole snug; the hole should be ⅜" to ½" shorter than the nail is long.

1. Butt one tray end A against the 8 ½" side of the feeder tray. Using a ⅛" bit, drill pilot holes, and attach tray end A to the feeder tray with galvanized nails.
2. Repeat step 1 to attach the remaining tray end A.
3. Using the same method, attach the tray sides B to the 12" side of the feeder tray, drilling pilot holes and nailing in place with the galvanized nails.

Adding the Roof Supports

NOTE: The roof supports are installed at a slant.

1. Turn the tray on its side and arrange one roof support C, in one corner on the inside of the tray. Mark the location on the underside of the tray. Drill a pilot hole, at a slant, through the underside into the center of the roof support. Nail in place from the bottom.

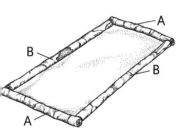

#2

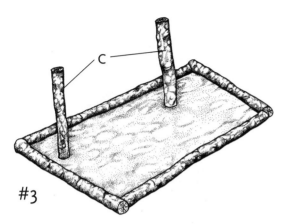

#3

2. Repeat to attach the remaining three roof supports.

Adding the Roof Peak Braces and the Ridge Pole

1. Place the construction upright on the work surface. Center the forked roof peak brace D, between two side roof supports C. Trim the roof peak brace D where it forks, if necessary. Allow the ends of the roof peak brace to overlap the roof supports 2" to 4". This will help to keep the seed dry.
2. Butt the ridge pole F, between the two roof peak braces. Drill pilot holes, and nail in place. This helps to stabilize the construction.
3. Weave the vines under and over the side roof braces C, and the ridge pole F, filling in tightly. Check your progress as you go along and push each row of weaving close together to ensure a tight roof.

To hang the bird feeder, tie a 20" length of rope or wire around both roof side braces. For another hanging option, drill a hole through the ridge pole, at the center, and screw in a screw-eye, and tie the wire or rope through the screw-eye.

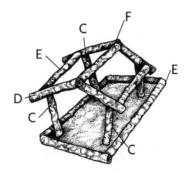

forked roof
peak brace D

#4

Suet
Feeder

THIS SIMPLE PROJECT IS A GREAT way for beginners to get
started. Hanging in your winter garden and filled with Bird Seed
Pudding, this feeder will attract chickadees, nuthatches, and
winter cardinals. To make old fashioned Bird Seed Pudding: Mix
¼ cup melted suet with ¾ cup bird-seed (including peanuts,
millet and sunflower seeds); press into feeder openings, and
place in a cool place or refrigerator to set. Hang it outside for
your wildlife friends.

MATERIALS   *Skill Level: beginner*
Choose a hardwood such as white birch, beech, cedar, or hickory.
The suet feeder requires a branch 12" long and 2" to 3" in diam-

143

eter. Four twigs, 6" long or eight twigs, approximately 3" long and ¼" to ½" in diameter will be needed for the perches.

TOOLS
- Crosscut hand saw
- Ruler or measuring tape
- Marking pencil
- Vise
- Electric drill with a selection of bits
- Wood glue (optional)
- Galvanized metal screw-eye and rope, or leather lace for hanging
- Safety goggles
- Work gloves

DIRECTIONS
1. Cut off all protruding branches from a 12" branch, and sand the surface smooth if necessary. All perch holes and suet holes are spaced approximately 1" from each other.
2. Using the diagram as a guide, measure and mark the locations where the holes are to be drilled.
3. Wrap the 12" branch with soft fabric such as terry cloth, to avoid crushing the branch while you are working with it in the vise.
4. Place it firmly in the vise. Using the correct size bit, drill holes approximately 1" in diameter for the suet openings, and ¼" for the perch. The perch holes may be drilled completely through the branch to accommodate the 6" twigs, or part way through for the 3" perches. If you choose the shorter version, use a dab of wood glue in each perch opening.
5. Add the galvanized metal screw-eye and rope for hanging.

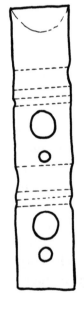

#1

CHAPTER 6

Furniture

The Willy Loveseat

*"Great pleasure was it to be there
Till green turned duskier and the moon
Coloured the corn-sheaves like gold hair."*

ALGERNON CHARLES SWINBURNE

A *WILLOWER* OR PERSON WHO WORKS WITH WILLOW WAS called a *Willy* in the Scottish Highlands and Northern English villages in the eighteenth century; therefore this classically designed loveseat is named *The Willy*. With its sturdy stretchers and high back it is perfectly at home on a porch, by poolside or in a garden. This practical piece, built in a weekend, is sure to be enjoyed for many years.

MATERIALS   *Skill Level: experienced*
Willow, hickory, birch, beech or any hardwood branches ranging in length from 13" to 36" in length and from ¾" to 1 ¾" in diam-

146

eter may be used for the basic structure. You will also need six-teen ¾" to 1" diameter branches, 36" long for the seat, along with a few pliable willow shoots for the back trim, and a peak-shape branch 37" long for the top rail. Galvanized flathead nails in as-sorted sizes (#4p, #6p, #8p, and #10p) and about three dozen 1" finishing nails are also required. You will need a 10" length of 1 1/16" or 1 1/8" straight wire for threading the top trim.

TOOLS
- Crosscut hand saw
- Single bit axe for felling trees
- Garden shears or clippers
- ⅜" variable-speed drill
- Measuring tape
- Marking pencil
- Hammer
- Safety goggles
- Work gloves

CUTTING CHART

Name of Part	Quantity	Diameter (inches)	Length (inches)	Description
Back legs A	2	1 ½	36	hardwood
Front legs B	2	1 ½	25	hardwood
Arms C	2	1 ½	17	hardwood
Beams D	5	1 ¾	32	hardwood
Front/back braces E	4	1–1 ¼	21	hardwood
Seat/back F	3	1–1 ¼	13	hardwood
Top rail G	1	¾	37	peaked, hardwood
Top trim H	8	½	1–21	hardwood
Side beams I	4	1–1 ¼	15–16	hardwood
Side braces J	4	1	18	hardwood
Seat support braces K	2	1 ½	16	hardwood
Seat L	16	¾–1	36	hardwood

DIRECTIONS

Cutting the Branches

1. Cut two 1 ½" diameter branches for the back legs A, each 36" long.

2. Cut two 1 ½" diameter branches for the front legs B, each 25" long.

3. Cut two 1 ½" diameter branches for the arms C, each 17" long.

4. Cut four 1 ¾" diameter branches for the beams D, each 32" long.

5. Cut four 1" to 1 ¼" diameter branches for the front/back braces E, each 21" long.

6. Cut three 1" to 1 ¼" diameter branches for the seat back F, each 13" long.

7. Cut one ¾" diameter peaked (bent or arched) branch 37" long for the top rail G.

8. Cut eight ½" diameter branches in graduated sizes from 1" to 21" for the top trim H.

9. Cut two 1" to 1 ¼" diameter branches for the side beams I, each 16" long.

10. Cut four 1" diameter branches for the side braces J, each 18" long.

Laying Out the Sub-Assembly

1. Butt one beam D between both back legs A, 3" up from the bottom of each leg. Using pilot hole construction, nail in place from the outside of each leg.

2. Butt one beam D between both back legs A, 13" up from the bottom beam. Nail in place as in step 1 above.

3. Butt one beam D between both back legs A, 5" from the top of the legs. Nail in place as before.

4. Butt one seat/back F between the two top back beams D, at the center (16" from either end). Drill holes from the top, and the bottom of the beams, and nail the F part in place.

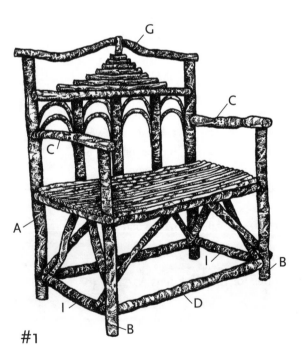

#1

5. Arrange the remaining seat/backs at approximately 8" on either side of the center seat/back. Using pilot hole and nail construction, nail in place as in diagram 7.

6. Butt one beam D between both front legs B, 3" up from the bottom of each leg. Nail in place as in step 1 above.

7. Butt the remaining beam D between both front legs B, 13" up from the bottom beam. Using pilot hole and nail construction, nail in place.

Joining the Sub-Assemblies

1. Butt top side beam I, between the inside of the front and back legs at the same points as the front and back beams D. Drill pilot holes and nail in place from the outside of the legs.

2. Repeat with the opposite side.

3. Butt bottom side beam I, between the inside front and back legs at approximately the same point that the front and back beams D meet the back legs. Drill pilot holes and nail in place from the outside of the legs.

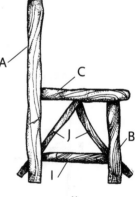

#2

4. Repeat with the opposite side.

5. Position one arm C across a front leg B, allowing it to extend approximately 1".
   From the top, drill pilot holes and nail arm C to leg B using a #8p nail.

6. Attach arm C to the back leg A at the spot where they meet. Drill a pilot hole from the back of the back leg, partway through arm C, and nail in place.

7. Repeat with the opposite side.

8. Lay the construction on its back. Position one front/back brace E along the (front) inner top beam D, and along the inside front leg approximately 6" from the bottom of the leg, resting it on the top of the side beam I.

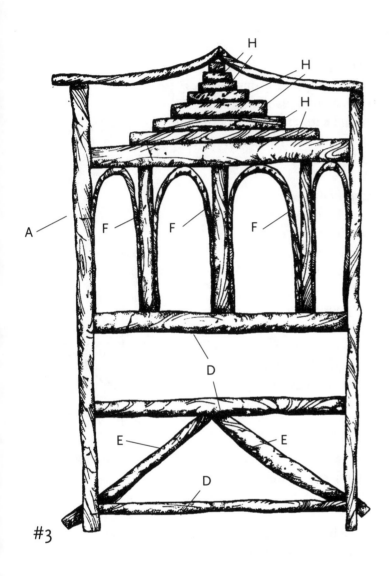

A

H
H
H

F   F   F

D

E   E

D

#3

9. Drill and nail brace E in place through the brace into the top beam D, and the front leg B.

10. Repeat with the opposite side.

11. Position one front/back brace E along the (back) inner top beam D, and along the inside back leg approximately 6" from the bottom of the leg, resting it on the top of the side beam.

12. Repeat steps 9 and 10 above with the remaining braces.

13. Add the side braces J to the inside top side beam I, and the inside of the lower back and front beams D.

Adding the Seat

1. Butt the two seat support braces K between the top front and back beams D, near each side seat back F. Using pilot hole construction, nail each part K to the back and front beams.

2. Stand the construction up.

Beginning at the back and working toward the front, position one seat branch L along the top of both top side beams I. Drill pilot holes and nail in place to the top side beams I, and the seat support braces K. Continue to drill and nail the remaining seat branches forming a tight fitting seat.

3. Trim the ends of the front seat branch for a tight fit between the two front legs.

Adding the Trim and Top Rail

1. Gently bend 25" to 30" lengths of pliable willow branches; form into an arch and install between the seat/back parts F, and the back legs as pictured.
2. Overlap the top rail G across the extended ends of the back legs A. Drill pilot holes and nail in place.

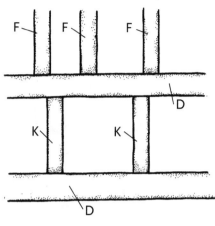

#4

3. Arrange top trim pieces H as pictured. At the center point drill completely through each part, and partway through the top beam D. Insert a 9" or 10" length of $\frac{1}{16}$" or $\frac{1}{8}$" straight wire in the drilled hole on the top beam D. Thread all top trim parts H on the inserted wire.
4. Drill a hole partway through the top rail G under the center peak. Arrange the center peak in place on the wire, trimming the wire if necessary; overlap the top rail G across the extended ends of the back legs A. Drill pilot holes and nail in place.

A handsome piece of furniture, complete in itself, The Willy Loveseat is surprisingly comfortable—it is built to help you enjoy the view. Add a few cozy calico or cotton duck pillows if you are using it in a covered area. The slight color variations of the wood seem to improve with time when the piece is left in its natural state. If, however, you choose to paint it, consider using a distinctive shade of green such as sage or bayberry to complement your outdoor area.

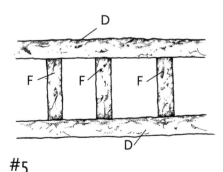

#5

Cedar & Vine Garden Bench

"When I discovered a new plant, I sat down beside it for a minute or a day, to its acquaintance and hear what it had to tell … "
JOHN MUIR

I DECIDED TO MAKE THIS BENCH WHEN A MASS OF VIRGINIA creeper vine was cut to make way for a new pond on a neighbor's property. I hated to see such a mother lode go to waste, and enlisted help to wrap, twist, and fasten the flexible vine on the garden bench before it dried. The materials dictated the design, and I hope it will inspire your rustic imagination.

MATERIALS *Skill Level: experienced*
Cedar, willow, hickory, or any pliable branches ranging from 20" to 95" in length, and 1 ½" to 2 ½" in diameter may be used for the basic structure. A flexible (green) length of vine is used for the wrapped loops; however, a selection of pliable branches, as

long as possible and ¼" to ½" in diameter may be substituted. You will also need a 1 ½" thick board, 16" × 54" for the seat. Two or three boards nailed together may be used for the seat. Galvanized flathead nails in assorted sizes (#4p, #6p, #8p, #12p, and #16p) and a few handfuls of 1" finishing nails will be required. The following directions are for the basic construction. Design your own back and fill in with available materials.

TOOLS

- Single bit axe for felling trees
- Crosscut hand saw
- ⅜" variable-speed drill
- Measuring tape
- Marking pencil
- Hammer
- Clippers or garden shears
- Safety goggles
- Work gloves
- Pocket knife (optional)

CUTTING CHART

Name of part	*Quantity*	*Diameter (inches)*	*Length (inches)*	*Description*
Back legs A	2	2	33–36	pliable, hardwood
Front leg B	1	2	30	pliable, hardwood
Curved front leg B1	1	2	34	pliable, hardwood
Top side beams C	2	1 ½	21	hardwood
Bottom side beam D	2	1 ½	23	hardwood
Arm E	1	1 ½	27	hardwood
Arm/back wrap E1	1	1–1 ½	95	pliable, hardwood
Bottom braces F	3	1 ¼–1 ¾	55	pliable, hardwood
Leg-to-leg, or Leg-to-seat brace G	2	¾–1 ½	20	pliable, hardwood

DIRECTIONS

Cutting the Branches

1. Cut two 2" diameter branches for the back legs A, 33" to 36" long. NOTE: The length of the back legs vary because one, or

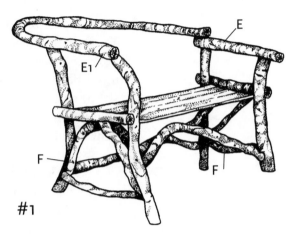

#1

both may splay outward during construction. It is better to cut the longer version and trim when necessary.

2. Cut one 2" diameter branch for the front leg B, 30" long.

3. Cut one 2" diameter branch for the curved front leg B1, 34" long, remembering to allow for the slight bending and trimming that may be required.

4. Cut two 1 ½" diameter branches for the top side beams C, each 21" long.

5. Cut two 1 ½" diameter branches for the bottom side beams D, each 23" long.

6. Cut one 1 ½" diameter branch for the arm E, 27" long.

7. Cut one 1" to 1 ½" diameter flexible branch for the arm/back wrap E1, 95" long.

8. Cut three (or more) 1 ¼" to 1 ¾" diameter pliable branches for the bottom braces F, each 55" long.

9. Cut two ¾" to 1 ½" diameter pliable branches for the leg-to-seat (or leg-to-leg) braces G, each 20" long.

10. Cut one, or more pieces of 1 ½" thick lumber 54" long and measuring 16" deep.

11. Have an assortment of vine, or flexible twigs ready to create the back support.

Laying Out the Basic Construction

1. Overlap side beam C across back leg A and front leg B 18" to 19" up from the bottom of both legs on the outside. The beam

will extend approximately 1" beyond both legs.

2. Join beam C to the legs using a #12p nail.

3. Overlap top side beam C across back leg A and curved front leg B1 18" to 19" up from the bottom of both legs on the outside. The beam will extend approximately 1" beyond both legs. Using pilot hole construction, nail as in step 2 above.

4. Position the seat between both leg/beam assemblies, and with pilot hole construction attach the seat to the top side beams C, through the outside of the beams. Make sure the seat is level at this step.

5. Lay arm E on top of front leg B and its corresponding back leg A. The arms should extend about 2" beyond the front and back of the legs. Make sure the back of the arm is long enough to support the arm/back wrap E1.

6. Drill holes through the arm and into the top of the legs at the point where they meet. Nail in place using #8p or #10p nails.

7. Lay arm/back wrap E1 on top of the curved front leg B1. The arm extends 2" to 3" beyond the curved front leg. Drill a hole through the arm and into the top of the front leg B1 at the point where they meet. Nail in place with pilot hole and nail construction.

8. Carefully place arm/back part E1 on top of its corresponding back leg A, and nail in place.

9. Continue to gently move the extended E1 part into a pleasing shape with its end resting on top of the

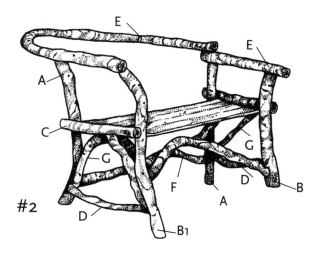

#2

installed arm E, thus forming the back rest as pictured. Nail
E1 to E at the point where they meet.

10. Butt bottom side beam D between the front and back legs
approximately 5" up from the bottom. Nail in place using a
#10p, or #12p nail. Repeat with the opposite side.

Bracing and Completing

The braces strengthen and help to support the structure. Add as
many as you feel are needed for your design.

1. Place one bottom brace F between both back legs
approximately 7" up from the bottom. Drill and nail in place
from the outside.

2. Because the bottom braces F are longer than the length of
the bench, the braces will arch upward when placed between
the legs. Arrange a bottom brace F along the inside of both
back legs. Drill and nail in place along the inside.

3. Repeat with the remaining bottom brace between the inside
of both front legs.

4. Add the remaining 20" braces G from leg to leg, or leg to the
underside of the seat as required for added stability.

5. Wrap, weave, loop, and arrange the vines, or twigs between
the arm/back wrap E1, and the seat to create a sturdy back
support. Drill pilot holes and nail in place to E, E1, and the
seat, with finishing nails, where needed.

Garden

Chair

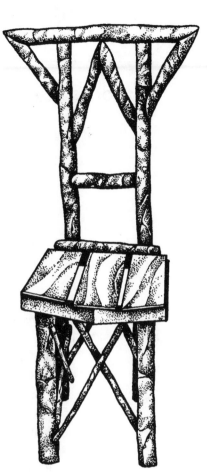

*"The garden is the place I
go to for refuge and shelter,
not the house."*

ELIZABETH & HER GERMAN
GARDEN, MAY 16, 1880

GARDEN SEATS, WITH THEIR DECORATIVE VALUE, ARE
appreciated by the gardener who takes the time to sit and think.
Add this straightforward chair to your garden scene and stop to
enjoy the view.

MATERIALS   *Skill Level: intermediate*
You will need hardwood branches such as willow, cedar, beech,
or birch. Lengths will range from 7" to 36", and diameters from
¾" to 2". You will also need a piece of lumber 3 ¾" wide × 42"
long. Galvanized flathead nails in assorted sizes (#4p, #6p, #8p,
and #10p) common nails, and finishing nails are required.

TOOLS
- Single bit axe for felling trees
- Crosscut hand saw
- Coping saw
- Clippers
- Ruler or measuring tape
- Marking pencil
- Drill with a selection of bits
- Hammer
- Miter box (optional)
- Safety goggles
- Work gloves

CUTTING CHART

Name of Part	Quantity	Diameter (inches)	Length (inches)	Description
Back legs A	2	1 ¾–2	36	hardwood
Back seat support B	1	1	12	hardwood
Front seat support C	1	1	12	hardwood
Front legs D	2	1 ¾–2	16	hardwood
Seat boards	3	3 ¾-wide × 14 long ea.		lumber
Crossed leg braces E	8	¾	13–15	hardwood
Back stretcher F	1	1	7	hardwood
Top beam G	1	1	19	hardwood
End fretwork H	2	1	9	hardwood
Center fretwork I	2	1	9	hardwood
Back legs trim J	1	¾	11	hardwood
Seat trim K	4	1 ¼	7 ½–13	split/hardwood

DIRECTIONS

Cutting the Branches

1. Cut two 1 ¾" to 2" diameter branches for the back legs A, each 36" long.
2. Cut one 1" diameter branch for the back seat support B, 12" long.
3. Cut one 1" diameter branch for the front seat support C, 12" long.
4. Cut two 1 ¾" to 2" diameter branches for the front legs D, each 16" long.

5. Cut eight ¾" diameter branches for the front leg braces E, each 13" to 15" long.
6. Cut one 1" diameter branch for the back stretcher F, 7" long.
7. Cut one 1" diameter branch for the top beam G, 19" long.
8. Cut two 1" diameter branches for the end fretwork H, each 9" long.
9. Cut two 1" diameter branches for the center fretwork I, each 9" long.
10. Cut one ¾" diameter branch for the back legs trim J, 11" long.
11. Split two 1 ¼" diameter branches, and cut 7 ½" to 13" long for the seat trim K.
12. Cut three ¾" thick and 3 ¾" wide seat boards 14" long for the seat.

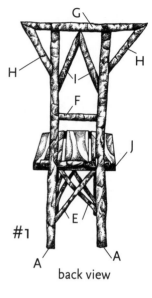

#1 back view

Laying Out the Sub-Assembly

1. Begin construction from the back. Lay out the two back legs A parallel, approximately 8" apart on the workbench. Mark a point 15" from the bottom of both back legs. At the 15" mark overlap the back seat support B across both legs (1" to 2" of part B will extend beyond the legs). Drill a pilot hole through part B into part A, and nail in place.

2. Place the two front legs D, parallel and approximately 8" apart on the workbench. Overlap the front seat support C across both legs 16" from the bottom of both legs; the seat will rest on top of the front (and the back) seat supports. Attach part C to the front legs D, using pilot hole and nail construction.

Making the Seat

Refer to the seat slat cutting diagram 3.

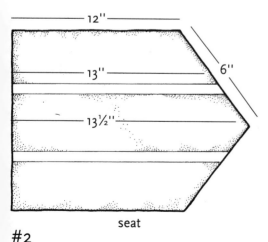

12"
13"
6"
13½"

seat

#2

1. NOTE: Back seat support B and front seat support C are placed inside the construction. Place the center precut seat slat on top of the back seat support B; nail in place from the top of the seat. Turn the construction over on the workbench and make a mark 9" from the back seat support B. Join the front sub-assembly to the seat slat at that location using pilot hole construction from the seat top.

2. Position one side precut seat slat along the back and front seat supports. Drill pilot holes and nail seat slats to front and back seat supports, C and B as above.

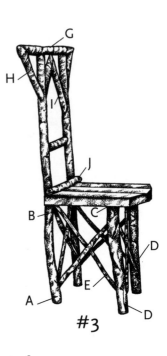

#3

3. Repeat step 2 with the remaining seat slat.

4. Butt back stretcher F between the back legs 23" from the bottom. Drill pilot holes and nail in place from the outside of legs A.

5. Place seat beam J across the seat slats, overlapping back legs A. Using pilot hole construction, nail in place through seat beam J and back legs A.

Adding the Crossed Leg Braces

1. To add the *front-to-back* leg braces E, nail from the inside front leg, 4" from the bottom to the back seat support on both sides.

2. To add the *back-to-front* leg braces E, nail from the inside back leg 4" from the bottom (overlapping the installed cross brace), to a location on the inside of the front leg approximately 12" from the bottom.

3. To add the *back-to-back* leg braces E, nail from the inside of

one back leg, 4" from the bottom to the outside of the opposite back leg. This will be at a location close to where the seat meets the back legs. Repeat with an additional crossed brace, overlapping the first.

4. To add the *front-to-front* leg braces E, attach one crossed leg brace E from the front of the front seat support C, to a front leg A, approximately 2" to 3" from the bottom of the leg. Repeat with the last remaining leg brace, overlapping the first.

Adding the Fretwork and Seat Trim

1. Position top beam G, across the top of the back legs A. Drill through both pieces and nail in place through the top of part G into parts A.
2. Refer to diagram 1, and arrange the end fretwork pieces H, beveling the ends with the coping saw. NOTE: Using a miter box helps to cut the angle to join the parts.
3. Refer again to diagram 1 and lay out the end fretwork pieces H. Mark for nail placement by placing a pencil dot on the top beam and the fretwork piece.
4. Drill and nail end fretwork H to the top beam G, and to the outside of leg A, as pictured.
5. Repeat with opposite side.
6. Arrange center fretwork I. Mark the pieces for nail placement as in step 3 above.
7. Begin with both center fretwork pieces and join them together at their junction point. Now fit the I assembly in place and join to the back legs at the pencil marks, remembering pilot hole construction.
8. Bevel the ends of the front split branch seat trim parts K as in step 2 above. Arrange the front seat trim in place and nail to the seat.
9. Arrange side seat trim in place (with mitered corners meeting), and nail in place.

Gothic Arm Chair

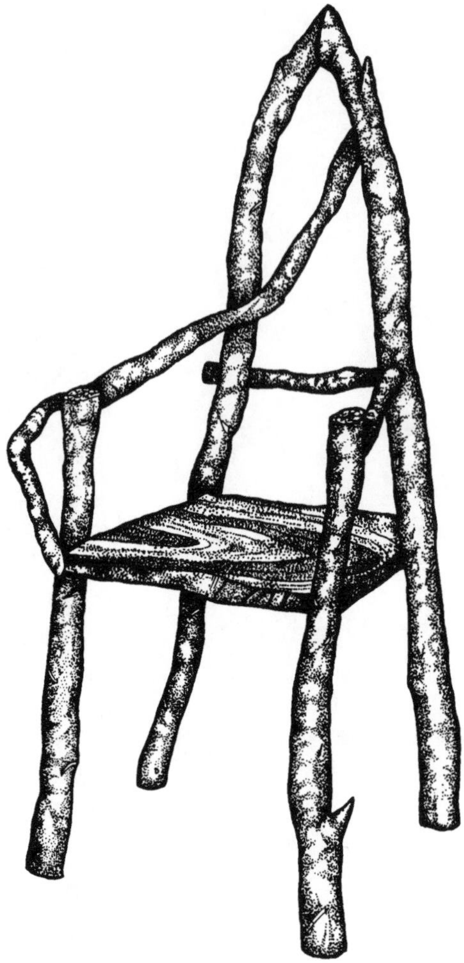

"I love it, I love it; and who shall dare
To chide me for loving that old arm-chair?"

ELIZA COOK, 1818–1889

TAKING A CUE FROM HISTORICAL EUROPEAN GARDENS, this gothic inspired arm chair is sure to become a favorite. The intimate connection between tree and furniture becomes obvious when you notice how few limbs are needed for this project. You will have to alter the design somewhat to accommodate your particular branches, but the plans are easy to adapt and you will want to make this sculptural chair for your retreat or garden.

MATERIALS

Skill Level: experienced

Use such woods as beech, cedar, cherry, or maple. Lengths will range from 25" to 47" and 1" to 2" in diameter for the chair, and ¾" diameter branches, 10" to 15" long for the trim. You will want to have a good selection of multi-branched and forked pieces, for it is in this combination of parts that a unique chair will be built. Trees at the edge of dense woods are often bent into distorted shapes in their fight for survival, and the natural twists and turns of their branches are what you want to add grace and style to your design. One or two pieces of 1 ½" pine, totaling 13" × 16" will be required for the seat. Have a selection of galvanized flat-head nails, 1 ½" galvanized roofing nails, and 1 ½" finishing nails, and you are ready to begin.

TOOLS

- Single bit axe for felling trees
- Crosscut hand saw
- Clippers or garden shears
- Ruler or measuring tape
- Marking pencil
- Drill with a selection of bits
- Hammer
- Safety goggles
- Work gloves

CUTTING CHART

Name of Part	Quantity	Diameter (inches)	Length (inches)	Description
Back legs/back A	2	1–2	47	Hardwood

NOTE: The following part B is more than one piece; the arms are graceful branches growing out of the leg. The chair's left front leg is 26" long, and its extended (attached) wraparound arm is 22" long. The right front leg is 26" long and forked; its extended (attached) wraparound arm/backrest is 24" long.

Name of Part	Quantity	Diameter (inches)	Length (inches)	Description
Front legs/arms B	2	1–2	47–51	Natural forked & bent
Seat trim C	5	½–1	10–16	Willow (or any hardwood)

NOTE: The seat measures 16" at the front edge and 13" at the back.

Name of Part	Quantity	Diameter (inches)	Length (inches)	Description
Seat	1	1 ½" thick	13 × 16	Pine (or scrap wood)

DIRECTIONS   *Cutting the Basic Branches*

1.   Carefully select two similarly shaped 1" to 2" diameter branches for the back legs/back A, each approximately 47" long, allowing for final leg trimming, and the arched construction.

2.   Carefully select two natural forked and curved branches for the front legs/arms B, each approximately 47" to 51" long, allowing for trimming and fitting.

Building the Back

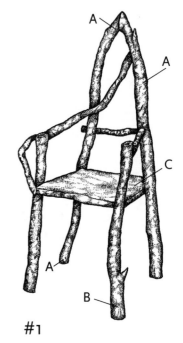

#1

1.   Using a pencil, mark the inside of both back legs A, 17" from the bottom.

2.   Position the seat (13" end) between the two back legs A at the pencil marks (17" from the bottom). NOTE: You will probably have to cut a curve out of the back seat corners to fit the back legs in place.

3.   Drill pilot holes and nail back legs to the seat.

4.   Slightly bend legs/back parts A at the top; slice at an angle and fit together, forming the gothic arch. Drill pilot holes and nail in place.

Adding the Front Legs/Arms

1.   Using a pencil, mark the inside of both front legs/arms B, 17" from the bottom. NOTE: The arms branch from the legs at approximately 7" above the seat.

2.   Position the seat (16" end) at the 17" front leg/arm point. Drill pilot holes and nail in place. Adjust the extending arm

in place, and attach it with pilot hole and nail construction at a point where it naturally crosses a back member.

3. Repeat with remaining front leg/arm B.

Adding the Seat Trim

1. Cut two ½" diameter twigs, 13" long for the side seat trims C.
2. Adjust the side seat trims C to fit, using three finishing nails each. Drill and nail in place from the front with pilot hole and nail construction.
3. Repeat with the opposite side.
4. Cut one 1" diameter twig, 16" long for the front seat trim C. Adjust to fit, and nail in place as in step 2 above.

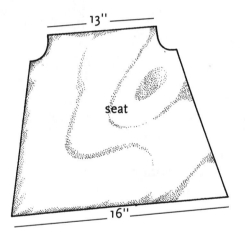

#2

Revamped Rocking Chair

*"To make good use of
idle time in the winter,
when there is but little to do
in the garden,
cut the wood for rustic chairs and tables."*

PETERSON'S MAGAZINE, NOVEMBER, 1856

A ROCKING CHAIR IS PERFECT IN THE FLOWER GARDEN—
I just wish I had thought of it sooner! Gleaned from a yard sale,
this timeworn treasure takes on new life with a simple twig-
stringing technique. Once you discover how easy it is to repair
chairs with this method, you will be searching for forgotten
pieces to turn into tomorrow's heirlooms. Build the jig and adjust
the spacing for your particular chair; for the seat only, for the back
only, or for seat and back as in the rocker pictured.

MATERIALS
Skill Level: intermediate
NOTE: The following materials are for the specific chair illustrated. This antique chair originally had a caned back and seat, and therefore has pre-drilled holes along the rim surrounding the back and the seat. The threaded twig wires are inserted through these holes.

Use such wood as willow, beech, birch, or hickory. You will need 32 straight twigs, 15" long and 1" in diameter for the back. You will need 15 straight twigs, 16" to 21" long and 1" in diameter for the seat. You will also need four straight wires, approximately 30" long and ⅛" in diameter; two pieces of board, approximately 20" long to make the jigs; and one large nail to use with the jigs. Two forked 1" diameter branches are used for the arms.

TOOLS
- Axe or saw for cutting trees
- Crosscut hand saw
- Ruler
- Marking pencil
- Drill and a selection of bits
- Wire clippers

CUTTING CHART

Name of Part	Quantity	Diameter (inches)	Length (inches)	Description
Twigs (back)	32	½–¾	15	straight
Twigs (seat)	15	½–¾	16–21	straight
Arms	2	1	25	forked
Board (for jig)	1 or 2	21	any width	

DIRECTIONS
Cutting the Branches
1. Cut thirty-two branches 15" long, with diameters from ½" to ¾" for the back.
2. Cut fifteen branches 16" to 21" long with diameters from ½" to ¾" for the seat. NOTE: The length of the seat branches vary to accommodate the shape of the seat, while the back opening is uniform.

Making the Jig

1. One board can be used for both patterns. For the back, drill two holes 14" apart in a straight board that is at least 21" long. For the seat, drill two holes 17" apart in a straight board that is also at least 21" long.

Drilling the Branches

1. In 32 of the branches, drill holes 14" apart. Center them using the jig as your guide. (NOTE: To drill the second hole in each twig, place the nail in the first drilled hole through the jig into the branch. This holds the jig in place and ensures accuracy.) Make sure the diameter of the hole is large enough to allow you to thread the wire through the hole.
2. In 15 of the branches, drill holes 17" apart. Center them using the jig as your guide. Continue as in diagram 3.

Arranging the Back

1. Cut two straight wires to string the 32 back branches, leaving ten extra inches to allow for attaching the twigs to the chair.
2. String the 32 (back) drilled branches onto two straight pieces of wire. Place the first branch in the middle of both wires. Continue stringing from both directions equally, until all 32 branches are on the wires.
3. Bend the bare wire at each end of the threaded twigs, and insert the wires through the back rim chair holes at the top, and at the bottom of the back opening. To secure the wire end, form a knot, or hammer a nail part way on the back of the chair (near the wire end) and wrap the wire tightly around the nail. Using wire clippers, cut the ends of the wires.

Stringing the Twigs

1. String the drilled branches onto two straight pieces of wire. Place the first branch in the middle of both wires. Continue stringing from

#1

both directions equally, until the wire is
covered with enough branches to fully
cover the seat.

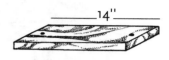

#2 jig for back

2. Bend the bare wire upward to form two
   U-shaped wires. There should be
   approximately 5" to 10" of wire at each end of the threaded
   twigs. These wire ends will be inserted in the chair's cane
   holes.

Arranging the Seat

1. Cut two straight wires to string the 15 seat branches, leaving
   ten extra inches to allow for attaching the twigs to the chair.
2. String the 15 (seat) drilled branches onto two straight pieces
   of wire. Follow the shape of the seat when stringing the seat
   branches, allowing for slight curves.
3. Bend the bare wire at each end of the threaded twigs, and
   insert the wires through the seat rim chair holes at the front,
   and at the back of the seat opening. Secure the wire ends in
   the same manner as the back wire ends (step 3 above).

jig for seat

#3

Adding the Arms

The one-piece forked branch that makes up the arm is attached
to the chair back at a convenient location, approximately 9" up
from the seat; and to the seat side-front at approximately 10" up
from the leg bottom.

Folding Bench

PERFECT FOR GARDENERS WITH LIMITED SPACE, THIS practical folding bench is easily stored when not in use. Amid a flower garden, topped with a wooden plank it is ideal for a summer picnic. Whether you use it to support bushel baskets when you are gathering your garden bounty, or to hold potted geraniums on the porch, I know you will want to try your hand at a rustic twig folding bench.

MATERIALS   *Skill Level: experienced*
Use straight hardwood branches such as birch, cedar, hickory, or willow. Lengths will range from 17" to 44" and diameters from 1 ¼" to 1 ¾". Three wood dowels, 16" long and ¾" to 1" in diameter

are required for the construction, along with galvanized flathead nails in assorted sizes.

TOOLS
- Single bit axe for felling trees
- Crosscut hand saw
- Clippers
- Ruler or measuring tape
- Marking pencil
- Hammer
- Drill with a selection of bits
- Safety goggles
- Work gloves

CUTTING
CHART

Name of Part	Quantity	Diameter (inches)	Length (inches)	Description
Top beams A	3	1 ¼–1 ¾	44	straight, hardwood
Legs B	4	1 ¼–1 ¾	21	straight, hardwood
Top rail C	2	1–1 ½	20	straight, hardwood
Bottom rail C1	2	1–1 ½	17	straight, hardwood
Wood dowels	3	¾–1	16	

DIRECTIONS

Cutting the Branches

1. Cut three 1 ¼" to 1 ¾" diameter straight branches for the top beams A, each 44" long.
2. Cut four 1 ¼" to 1 ¾" diameter straight branches for the legs B, each 21" long.
3. Cut two 1" to 1 ½" diameter straight branches for the top rails C, each 20" long.
4. Cut two 1" to 1 ½" diameter straight branches for the bottom rails C1, each 17" long.
5. Cut three ¾" to 1" diameter wood dowels 16" long.

Laying Out the Sub-Assemblies

NOTE: The top beams A are the "stops" that permit the bench to stand upright, and must extend beyond the top rails C when dowel

#1

joined. For this project you will want to read
all directions before beginning.

1. Place the three top beams A on the workbench.
    Using the pencil, mark a location at the center (22") on each
    beam.
2. Using the drill and correct bit, drill a hole with the same
    diameter as the dowel at each 22" mark .
3. Arrange the three top beams A, parallel on the workbench
    approximately 8" apart. Insert the dowel through all three
    top beams. Drill pilot holes and nail the dowel in place
    through the A beams, from the bottom. Set the top sub-
    assembly aside.
4. Place two legs B, parallel on the workbench approximately
    15" apart. Overlap one top rail C across both legs 3" to 4"
    down from the top of the legs. Drill pilot holes and nail in
    place.
5. Overlap bottom rail C1 across both legs 11" from the bottom
    of both legs. Drill pilot holes and nail in place.
6. Repeat steps 4 and 5 with the remaining legs B, and rails C
    and C1.

Joining the Sub-Assemblies

1. Place one leg assembly on the workbench along with the top
    assembly. Position the two legs B inside the two exterior top

beams A, and check to make sure that the three top beams rest on top of the top rail C. NOTE: The top rails are the "stops" that permit the bench to stand upright.

2. Using a pencil mark a spot along legs B, 1 ½" to 2" from the top. Drill a hole ⅛" larger than the diameter of a dowel at these spots.

3. Repeat steps 1 and 2 above with the remaining leg assemblies.

4. At a location 3" from the ends of the middle top beam A, drill holes ⅛" larger than the dowel's diameter. Remember, drilling the holes ⅛" larger than the diameter of the dowel makes folding the bench easy.

5. Position the legs B, inside the exterior top beams and insert the dowel through the three drilled holes. Try folding the legs at this point to make sure they move easily. Correct the drilled hole diameter if necessary. When you are satisfied with the placement, turn the construction over and nail the dowels in place through the top beams using pilot hole construction. Repeat with the opposite side.

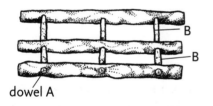

dowel A

#2   top view

Snack Table

*"April brings the primrose sweet,
Scatters daisies at
our feet."*
NURSERY RHYME

THIS IS SO EASY TO MAKE THAT YOU PROBABLY WILL DECIDE to make several for your outdoor parties. Plant them in the yard or along the garden path, to support a cool summer drink. Change the height to use it for a sun dial stand or a bird feeder station.

MATERIALS   *Skill Level: beginner*
You will need a log slice, 3" thick and approximately 13" in diameter. Log slices can be obtained from a logger, tree-trimming service, or firewood supplier. Thick planks of wood from a saw mill may be used as well. A 3" to 4" diameter log 25" to 40" long

is required for the leg, along with a #40p nail, or spike. Almost any wood may be used for the leg, such as birch, black locust, cedar, cypress, douglas fir, hickory, maple, oak, osage orange, pine, redwood, or spruce.

TOOLS
- Single bit axe for felling trees and for sharpening table leg
- Crosscut hand saw
- Sharp pocket knife (optional)
- Hammer
- Ruler or measuring tape
- Marking pencil
- Rubber maul, or mallet for driving table into the ground
- ⅜" variable-speed drill with a selection of bits
- Sandpaper (or electric sander)
- Safety goggles and work gloves

CUTTING CHART

Name of Part	Quantity	Diameter (inches)	Length (inches)	Description
Table top	1	12–13	3" thick	seasoned wood, such as pine, maple, hemlock, or oak
Table leg	1	3–4	25–40	seasoned wood, see materials above

DIRECTIONS

1. If you are lucky enough to have a tree stump near a wood pile, it is the perfect place to sharpen the end of the table leg. The bottom edge of the leg is cut in a six inch sharp angle. To make the bottom leg point, use the axe to hew off a thin piece at a time. Rotate the leg as you work, always working at the same angle. At 6" from the bottom, you should have achieved the desired sharp pencil point shape.
2. Prepare the wood slab by sanding the top surface smooth before the leg is installed.

3. Lay the slab top face down on a work surface. Using a marking pencil, mark the center of the slab. Drill a hole (slightly smaller than the #40p nail to allow for a snug fit) at the pencil mark.
4. Using the pencil, mark the center point on the top of the table leg. Drill a hole approximately 1" to 2" through the center point of the table leg.
5. Join the table leg to the table top with the #40p galvanized nail (or spike), through the pre-drilled holes.
6. Use a rubber (or rawhide) mallet to drive the snack table into the ground approximately 12" deep.

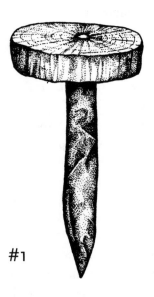

#1

Forked Garden Seat

"As violets recluse and sweet,
Cheerful as daisies unaccounted rare;
Still sunward gazing from a lowly seat;
Still sweetening wintry air."

CHRISTINA ROSSETTI

CRAFT THIS THREE-LEGGED FORKED-BACK CHAIR FROM AN appropriate branch and create a special resting spot in the garden. Easy to carry and well balanced, this chair fits almost anywhere and adds interest wherever it is placed. A descendant of the English walking chair, garden enthusiasts will welcome its simple design.

MATERIALS *Skill Level: beginner*
You will need three hardwood branches, including one forked branch, such as birch or beech, ranging from 18" to 40", and with

a 1 ½" diameter for leg A and a 1" diameter for legs B. You will also need a log slice, 2" thick and approximately 12" in diameter. NOTE: Log slices can be obtained from a logger, tree-trimming service, or firewood supplier. Thick wood planks from the lumber yard also work. You will also need wood glue for the front legs and two 1 ¾-inch finishing nails for the back leg.

TOOLS

- Single bit axe for felling trees
- Crosscut hand saw
- Ruler or measuring tape
- Marking pencil
- ⅜" variable-speed drill with a selection of bits
- Sandpaper (or electric sander)
- Wood glue (optional)
- Safety goggles and work gloves

CUTTING CHART

Name of Part	Quanity	Diameter (inches)	Length (inches)	Description
Back Leg A	1	1 ½	40	forked hardwood
Front Legs B	2	1	18	forked hardwood
Seat	1	12		2" thick seasoned wood, such as cherry, maple, pine, or oak

DIRECTIONS

1. Cut one forked 1 ½" diameter branch for the back leg A, 40" long.
2. Cut two 1" diameter branches for the front legs B, each 18" long.
3. Prepare the 12"-diameter wood slab by sanding the surfaces smooth.
4. Cut a U-shaped slice, approximately 1 ½" deep and 1 ½" wide, from the back of the wood slab seat to accommodate the back leg A, for a snug fit.

A

B

B

#1

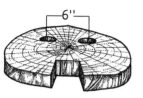

underside leg
placement

#2

Attaching the Front Legs to the Seat

1. Lay the slab-seat face down on a work table. Using a pencil, mark the slab at the two spots where the front legs will be inserted, 2 ½" in from the sides and 6" apart at approximately 3" from the seat front.
2. NOTE: Holes should be slightly smaller than the twig to allow for a snug fit. Drill holes approximately 1 ¼" deep at the pencilmarks.
3. Install legs in drilled holes and adjust as necessary to guarantee a level chair. At this point add a squirt of wood glue in the holes and a dab on the legs. Dip the legs in sawdust if they remain loose. Measure the legs to make sure they are of equal length, and adjust the bottoms if necessary.

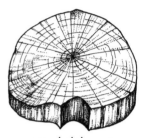

wood slab seat

#3

Attaching the Back Leg

With the construction remaining face-down permit the back to rest slightly over the edge of the work table. Position the back leg in the previously cut U-shaped seat back opening. The legs stand 16" to 17" tall from floor to seat—because the front legs splay slightly outward, they are approximately 17" and the back leg is approximately 16" tall.

Using pilot hole and nail construction, attach the back leg A, to the seat with two 1 ¾" finishing nails.

Stand the chair upright and trim the bottoms of the legs if necessary.

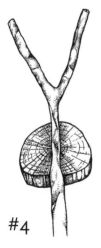

#4

back leg A

CHAPTER 7

A Baker's
Dozen
Quick & Easy
Projects

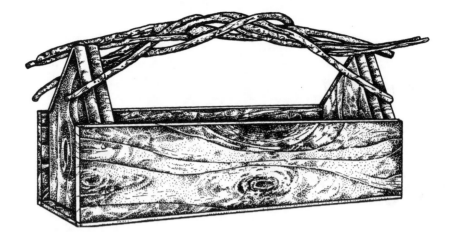

Twig-Handled Garden Tool Carrier

"Some morning in May I sit in the sunshine and soft air, transplanting my young Pansies and Gillyflowers into the garden beds ... "

CELIA THAXTER, AN ISLAND GARDEN

BUILT LIKE A CARPENTER'S TOOL BOX, THIS TWIG-HANDLED version is perfect for transporting your most frequently used items, such as a hand shovel, a weeder, your clippers, or your gloves. It is just as useful for carrying weeds to the compost pile, or greens to the kitchen, and it makes a nice planter.

MATERIALS   *Skill Level: beginner*

You will need five pieces of ½" to 1 ½" thick lumber in lengths from 9" to 25" and 5" wide. Almost any kind of wood may be used, from weathered barn siding to seasoned oak, or a good

182

quality pine from the lumber yard. The carrier pictured is made of old rough-sawed hemlock weathered to a nice silver gray color. You will also need an assortment of 30" long flexible twigs, with diameters from ¼" to ¾", along with galvanized flathead nails and 1" finishing nails.

TOOLS

- Crosscut hand saw
- Garden shears or clippers
- Ruler
- Pencil
- Drill with a selection of bits
- Hammer
- Safety goggles
- Work gloves

CUTTING CHART

Name of Part	Quantity	Length (inches)	Width (inches)	Description
Sides 1" thick A	2	25	5	Seasoned lumber
Bottom 1" thick B	1	25	5	Seasoned lumber
Ends 1 ½" thick C	2	9	5	Seasoned lumber
Handle D	1	22	¾-diam.	Pliable twig
Handle wraps E	4–6	30	¼–½	Pliable twigs
Trim F	4	5 ½	1-diam.	Hardwood twig/split

DIRECTIONS

Cutting the End Pieces

1. Measure 5" from the bottom of an end piece C, and using a pencil, mark both sides at this point. Repeat with the second end piece.
2. With the ruler and pencil, divide an end piece in half, and draw a line from top to bottom. Repeat with the second end piece.

#1

C   Trim F

B

A

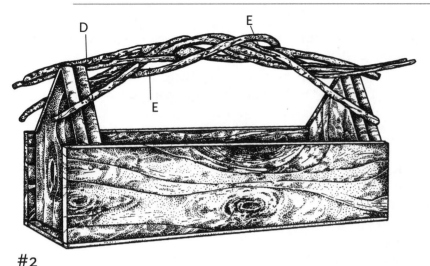

D

E

E

#2

3. Cut one end piece, at a slant from the top mid-point line to the 5" pencil mark. Repeat with the other side, forming the triangular top shape. Repeat with the remaining end piece.

Building the Carrier

1. Arrange one end piece C along the bottom B, allowing approximately ¾" of the bottom to extend. Join the end to the bottom, with pilot hole and nail construction, from the underside with 1 ½" galvanized nails (or any nails of choice guaranteeing a tight joint).
2. Repeat with the other end piece on the opposite side. NOTE: The sides overlap the end pieces and extend approximately ¾".
3. Join one side A, to an end piece with three 1 ½" galvanized nails, drilling pilot holes through the sides into the end piece. Repeat with the remaining side.

Adding the Handle and the Trim

1. Measure the inside distance between both ends C. Cut a ¾" pliable branch slightly shorter (approximately two inches shorter) than the inside distance. This permits the handle's shape to be formed.
2. Make a mark approximately 1" down from the top of both ends C, on the inside and on the outside. Join the handle at the mark, using pilot hole and nail construction, nailing from the outside. Carefully bend the handle to be joined at the

other end; taper the pliable twig to fit flush with the end if necessary, and join as above.

3. Cut two 1" diameter twigs approximately 5 ½" long for the trim F. Split in half, and attach to the triangle end pieces with pilot hole and nail construction and finishing nails. Repeat with the remaining ends.

4. Carefully bend ¼" to ¾" flexible twigs over and under the attached handle, permitting the twig ends to extend beyond the carrier., Tack some of these in place using thin finishing nails others will be able to stay put once they dry.

Star
Pocket
Planter

THIS LITTLE STAR POCKET PLANTER HELPS TO PRESERVE A
winter memory of a woodland walk where sheets of fallen birch
bark were brought home and applied to scrap wood. It is a
charming front door decoration holding dried herbs and grasses,
or add hemlock boughs and pinecones for a festive winter wall-
hanging.

MATERIALS   *Skill Level: intermediate*
You will need an assortment of peeled bark sheets, with two
sheets at least 11" wide (see pattern); and two pieces of scrap lum-

186

ber, each 11" × 11". One straight branch, at least 7" long is required, along with epoxy glue (or a glue gun) and ½" finishing nails.

TOOLS
- Clippers or garden shears
- Keyhole saw and coping saw
- Scissors
- 1" wide straight chisel (required for bark peeling)
- Wooden mallet (required for bark peeling)
- Ruler or measuring tape
- Marking pencil
- Hammer
- Work gloves

DIRECTIONS

Applying the Bark

1. Enlarge the pattern to the desired size. Trace both outlines, front and back, of the star pattern on the scrap lumber, and using the coping saw, cut out both shapes.
2. Trace the star outlines on the bark, and cut the bark with scissors.
3. Trace the triangle opening on the lumber and on the bark, and using the keyhole saw cut out both openings (this is for hanging the planter).
4. Lay back star face up on a work surface. Attach the bark to the star with the glue or glue gun. Affix bark to the front star with glue or glue gun.

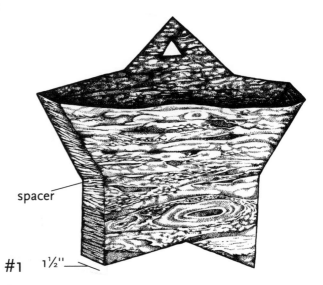

spacer

#1   1½"

Forming the Pocket

1. Cut ¼" diameter twig into seven 1" slices.
2. Place the 1" spacer twigs along the outside edge of the back star (see diagram) and using the finishing nails, nail in place from the back.
3. Place the front "pocket" on top of the installed spacers, and nail in place.

Closing the Sides

1. Cut bark strips 1 ½" wide and as long as possible to go around the outside edge. Nail in place from the outside to the edge of the scrap lumber. Trim the bark, if necessary, to fit between the front and the back.

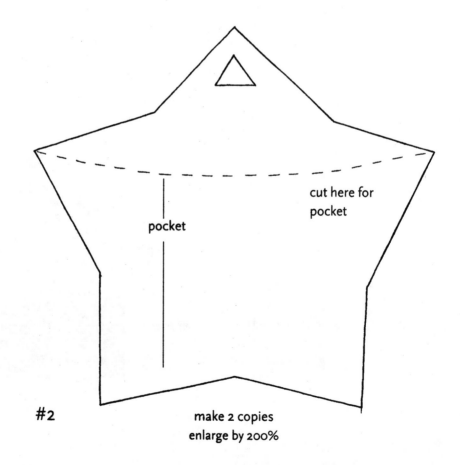

cut here for
pocket

pocket

#2

make 2 copies
enlarge by 200%

Garden
Markers

LABEL YOUR PLANTS THE NATURAL WAY WITH THESE whimsical markers that look as if they grew from the garden. The letters are formed with flexible twigs, and the stakes are whittled sticks. This is a good project for people with limited space and a welcomed gift for gardening friends.

MATERIALS

Skill Level: beginner
A walk in the woods can lead you to loose scraps of bark and appealing twigs that can be used for these garden markers. You will need a piece of scrap lumber, or a roofing shingle, and a 23" long twig for each marker. You will also need a piece of peeled birch

189

bark at least 3" wide and 6" long, along with a 23" long twig for the stake. Use pliable branches such as willow, alder, or hickory for the lettering. Lengths range from 3" to 24", and branch diameters should be ⅛" to ½" for the letters, and ¼" to ¾" for the trim, and ½" to 1 ½" for the stakes. You should also have a variety of tacks and finishing nails for attaching the bark veneer, twig trim and twig letters to the scrap lumber.

TOOLS

- Axe or saw for cutting trees
- Coping saw and/or keyhole saw
- Garden shears or clippers
- Sharp knife (optional)
- Scissors (for cutting bark)
- Ruler or measuring tape
- Marking pencil
- Drill with a selection of bits
- Tack hammer
- Staple gun (optional)
- Safety goggles
- Work gloves

DIRECTIONS

NOTE: The directions that follow are suggestions on materials, methods, and measurements; rely on your own design sense to create individualistic garden markers. The number of letters helps to determine the size of the marker, and the plants usually dictate the height. A good average is 3" × 6" for the markers, and 10" to 24" high for the stakes. The kale marker pictured is 3" × 6" and 12" high, while basil is 3 ½" × 4 ½" and 14" high.

1. Form the letters with supple twigs, and attach them to the wood boards with thin finishing nails. For an attractive variation, birch bark can be affixed to a wood foundation with carpet tacks before adding twig lettering.
2. Trim the board edges with twigs and fasten with finishing nails.

3. Fix the stakes on the back with galvanized flathead nails (#2p, #4p, or #6p).
4. Using a sharp knife, whittle one end of the stake into a point to permit easy installation.

Look at the illustrations for inspiration, but be willing to change your plans as the work progresses; it's all part of the creative experience.

#1

Handy Hooks

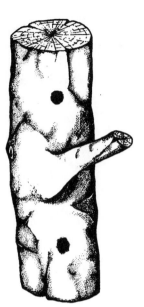

> *"Here in this sequestered close,*
> *Bloom the hyacinth and the rose;*
> *Here beside the modest stock*
> *Flaunts the flaring hollyhock;*
> *Here without pang, one sees*
> *Ranks, conditions, and degrees."*
>
> AUSTIN DOBSON

A PERFECT PLACE TO HANG YOUR GARDEN HAT, THESE handy natural branch hooks are simple to make. Install some in the potting shed to keep your tools off the floor and out of harm's way. Place some near the back door for aprons, smocks, and gardening clothes. Once you discover how these hooks help you tidy up your work area, you will be using them for lawn bags, watering cans, brooms, baskets, gloves, and the garden hose.

MATERIALS *Skill Level: beginner*

Choose a hardwood such as white birch, beech, maple, or cherry. All hooks require forked branches to form the natural peg. Individual handy hooks may vary in size from 8" to 12", with 1" to 2" diameters. The hooks are installed with two screws.

TOOLS
- Crosscut hand saw
- Ruler or measuring tape
- Marking pencil
- Electric drill and a variety of bits
- $\frac{1}{16}$" to $\frac{3}{8}$" woodboring bit (optional, needed to countersink drill the holes)
- Screwdriver for installation
- Safety goggles
- Work gloves

DIRECTIONS
1. Measure and mark the length of the branch in half. Using a hand saw, cut the branch in half along the mark.
2. Measure and mark two points 1" to 2" from the ends of the branch for the installation holes. Using the drill and bit, countersink both holes.

NOTE: To countersink a hole, drill a pilot hole slightly larger than the screw you plan to use. Countersunk holes are deeper than the length of the screw. After the screws are installed the holes may be plugged with pegs cut from twigs, thereby covering the screw heads.

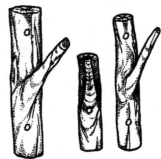

#1

Scarecrow

"In the further field
A scarecrow kept me company,
Walking as I walked."

SANIN, 17TH CENTURY HAIKU POET

ORIGINALLY USED TO FRIGHTEN crows or other birds away from crops, a scarecrow adds a bit of fanciful whimsy to any outdoor area. Scarecrows are easy to make out of twigs and branches with assorted found objects for facial features. This familiar figure is the perfect project for budding rustic designers looking for a garden centerpiece!

MATERIALS *Skill Level: beginner*

You will need a 3" thick wood slab, 13" in diameter for the head; two forked branches, 36" long for the arms; and one 90" long forked branch for the body (including the legs). Adjust the measurements to suit your location. Use three branches for the body/leg part if you cannot locate one forked branch. Consider

194

using one branch for the arms and adding multi-forked twigs for hands. Here a pair of buffing wheel brushes are used for the eyes and a brass hose nozzle for the nose. You will need a handful of galvanized nails to join the head and the arms to the body.

TOOLS

- Axe
- Crosscut hand saw
- Clippers or garden shears
- Ruler or measuring tape
- Marking pencil
- Drill with a selection of bits
- Hammer
- Safety goggles
- Work gloves

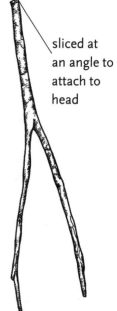

sliced at an angle to attach to head

#1

DIRECTIONS

#2

1. Place the wood slab (face) on the workbench. Mark the location for the eyes, 6" down and centered 5" apart. Drill holes and nail eyes in place. Bottle caps, jar lids, or political buttons make good eyes. Center nose on face and attach. The garden nozzle is attached with a nail. If you don't have an extra garden nozzle lying around, a twig makes a suitable nose. For the mouth, drill a 1 ½" diameter hole, centered and 3" from the bottom.
2. Cut a 10" long slice lengthwise from the top of the body (neck). Place the cut side against the back of the head, and nail in place with pilot hole construction using three nails.
3. Arrange the pair of arms on the back, at a point 15" down from the chin. Attach the arms to the body from the back with two or three nails and pilot hole construction.

Add vines for hair, or nail on an old straw hat. Dress as desired.

Birdbath
Stand

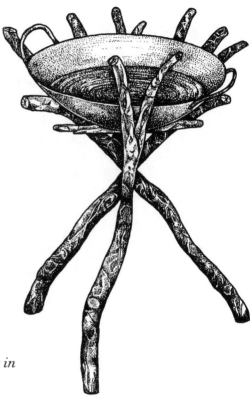

"And we'd be as happy as birds in the spring … "

WILLIAM BLAKE,
THE LITTLE VAGABOND

A BIRDBATH IS A DELIGHTFUL ADDITION TO ANY GARDEN and promises year-long enjoyment. This example, with its graceful proportions, is art for your garden. Use a sealed terra-cotta saucer, a discarded wok, or any shallow pan for the bath. For winter use, when birds need water for drinking, paint the inside of your birdbath with lead-free, flat black paint to stop the water from freezing and place in a sunny, windless area and fill with water. If the water in your birdbath does freeze, bring it indoors until it thaws out.

MATERIALS   *Skill Level: intermediate*
Three forked branches (any hardwood), approximately 42" long and 1 ½" in diameter, are required for the legs, and three hard-

wood branches 16" long and ½" to ¾" in diameter will be needed for the supports. You will also need galvanized flathead nails in assorted sizes (#4p, #6p, and #8p) along with a handful of finishing nails.

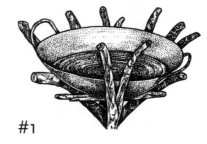

#1

TOOLS

- Single bit axe for felling trees
- Crosscut hand saw
- Clippers
- Ruler or measuring tape
- Marking pencil
- Hammer
- Drill with a selection of bits
- Safety goggles
- Work gloves

CUTTING CHART

Name of Part	Quantity	Diameter	Length	Description
Legs A	3	1 ½	42	forked, hardwood
Supports B	3	½–¾	16	hardwood

DIRECTIONS

Cutting the Branches

1. Cut three 1 ½" diameter hardwood branches for the legs A, each 42" long.
2. Cut three ½" to ¾" diameter branches for the supports B, each 16" long.

Building the Base

1. Check each of the three legs to make sure they will fit together in a pleasing arrangement just where the forks form. Try several compositions before deciding on your final design. If necessary, cut off any small branches that interfere.
2. Cross two legs at approximately 26" from the leg bottoms, forming an "X". Join the two legs A, together at this junction using pilot hole and nail construction.
3. Arrange the remaining leg, between the two joined legs

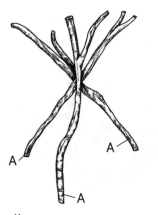

#2

through the top of the "X". Attach to the joined legs using the same construction technique.

4. Check for stability and adjust the ends, if necessary.

Adding the Supports

1. Drill a pilot hole approximately 4" from the end of one support B and through a point approximately 10" down from the top of one fork of a leg. Using pilot hole and nail construction, attach the support to the leg at this point.

2. NOTE: The supports are attached under and over each other, forming an equilateral triangle. To attach the second support B, place one end of the second support branch over the installed support and using pilot hole construction attach to the neighboring leg.

3. Attach the third support B, in the same manner as above.

4. Using pilot hole construction, join the supports to the legs at locations where they meet.

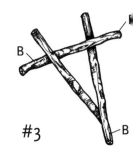

#3

Rest a clay saucer or any suitable vessel on the supports, allowing the extended legs to cradle it.

NOTE: To seal a terra-cotta saucer or a wok, apply several coats of marine waterproof varnish.

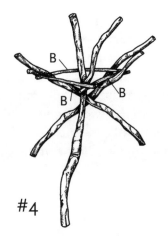

#4

Sundial
Stand

PLACE A PURCHASED SUNDIAL ON THIS SIMPLE STAND IN the midst of your garden, and you will always know what time it is. Based on early Gypsy designs, this easy stand is a good beginners project that will add interest to your landscape. Ground-hugging plants like mother-of-thyme or purslane are lovely planted at the base. Sundials may be purchased at garden supply shops, some hardware stores, and in many gift and gardening mail-order catalogues.

MATERIALS   *Skill Level: beginner*
Alder, cedar, mulberry, willow, or another similar wood may be used. Lengths range from 4" to 30", and diameters ¾" to 1 ¼". You will also need a ½" thick piece of scrap wood 12" × 12" for the top. #2p and #4p galvanized box nails are required (box nails are flathead nails, lighter in weight than common galvanized flathead nails).

TOOLS
- Single bit axe for felling trees
- Crosscut hand saw
- Clippers
- Ruler
- Marking pencil
- ⅜" variable-speed drill
- Hammer
- Safety goggles
- Work gloves

CUTTING CHART

Name of Part	Quantity	Diameter (inches)	Length (inches)	Description
Legs A	3	1	30	hardwood
Cross braces B	3	¾	12	hardwood
Edge trim C	4	1 ¼	4–5	split in half, hardwood
Top	1	½-thick	12 × 12	see diagram

DIRECTIONS   *Making the Top*

1. Cut ½" thick wood in the octagon shape as shown in diagram #2. Purchased sun dials often come in an octa-gonal shape.
2. Place the top face down on the workbench. Using the pencil make 3 marks approximately 2" from the edge at the three locations indicated on the diagram.
3. Split the four edge trim C parts in half lengthwise, thereby creating eight pieces.
4. Arrange the edge trim C, with split edge facing octagon table

top edges. Drill and nail in place using two to three nails at each location.

Adding the Legs

1. Arrange the legs, one at a time, using the leg placement diagram 1 as a guide. Drill pilot holes through the table top and nail legs in place. Legs cross at approximately 9" down forming the tripod.

Adding the Cross Braces

1. Attach cross braces B, at a slant, between neighboring legs with pilot hole and nail construction. See diagram for placement.
2. Stand the construction upright and check for stability. Adjust the leg botttoms, if necessary.

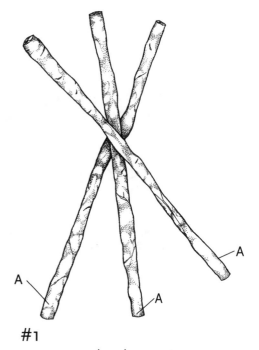

A

A

A

#1

leg placement

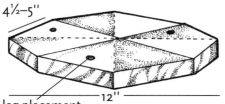

4½–5"

leg placement

12"

#2   top (underside)

Hanging
Herb & Flower
Drying Rack

"(Thymus vulgaris) Perennial. The green portion, either fresh or dried, is used extensively for flavoring soups, gravies, stews, etc. The leaves are easily dried in a shaded warm place. Pkt. 15 cts."

THIS SIMPLE HANGING RACK HELPS TO PRESERVE GARDEN herbs, fruits, and flowers. For tea blends, cooking, flower arrangements, and crafts, dried herbs are essential. Pick the flowers to be preserved on a dry morning, after the dew has settled. Tie them in small bundles and hang them upside down away from direct sunlight. Some of the herbs that dry most successfully in this manner are dill, lovage, the mints, oregano, parsley, rosemary, sage, tarragon, and thyme.

MATERIALS

Skill Level: beginner

You will want to choose straight but pliable branches of willow, alder, hickory, cedar, or another similar wood. Lengths will range from 10" to 21", and diameters from ¼" to 1". You will need one multi-forked branch for the hanger and a 1" diameter hardwood branch support bar. You will also need an assortment of finishing nails.

TOOLS

- Single bit axe for felling trees
- Crosscut hand saw
- Clippers or garden shears
- Ruler or measuring tape
- Marking pencil
- ⅜" variable-speed drill and a selection of bits
- Hammer
- Safety goggles
- Work gloves

CUTTING CHART

Name of Part	Quantity	Diameter (inches)	Length (inches)	Description
Hanger A	1	¼–¾	22	3-forked/pliable
Support bar B	1	1	19	straight
Pegs C	6	¼–½	10–12	straight

DIRECTIONS

Cutting the Branches

1. Cut one ¼" to ¾" diameter 3-forked twig for the hanger A, 22" long.
2. Cut one 1" diameter straight twig for the support bar B, 19" long.
3. Cut six ¼" to ½" diameter straight twigs for the pegs C, each approximately 11" long.

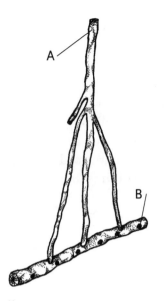

A

B

#1

Building the Rack

1. Position the 3-forked hanger A, along the top of the support bar B. Mark the three points where the branches meet the support bar.
2. Using the drill and correct bit for the three-forked hanger A, drill three holes half way through the support bar. Insert the hanger branches, and nail in place with finishing nails. This assures a secure fit.
3. Mark two points at 1 ½" in from both ends of the support bar B; and then mark points, evenly spaced, approximately 3" apart. Carefully drill holes (half way) for the correct peg diameters at these points.
4. Place the pegs snugly in the drilled holes. Use a dab of glue in the hole and a dab on the peg. If the peg is loose, dip it in sawdust and then insert it. Allow the hanging rack to dry thoroughly before using.

Herb &
Flower
Drying
Stand

"Open afresh your round of starry folds,
Ye ardent marigolds."
JOHN KEATS

GATHER YOUR FRESH HERBS BEFORE THE FIRST FROST, AND
hang them in bunches on this standing rack to dry. They will
help to scent and decorate your kitchen and your seasonings will
be close by. This adjustable rack folds up for out-of-season stor-
age. Its unique design is composed of four separate sections that
connect with metal screw-eyes from the hardware store.

MATERIALS

Skill Level: experienced

You will need five ¾" to 1" diameter straight branches for the legs, each 36" long; and twelve ½" to ¾" diameter straight branches for the rails, each 20" long. Nine 3" to 4" metal screw-eyes are required to join the sections, as well as an assortment of common nails.

TOOLS

- Single bit axe for felling trees
- Coping saw
- Crosscut hand saw
- Ruler
- Marking pencil
- Drill with a selection of bits
- Hammer
- Safety goggles

CUTTING CHART

Name of Part	Quantity	Diameter (inches)	Length (inches)	Description
Legs A	5	¾–1	36	straight/hardwood
Rails B	12	½–¾	20	straight/hardwood

DIRECTIONS

Cutting the Branches

1. Cut five ¾" to 1" diameter straight branches for the legs A, each 36" long.
2. Cut twelve ½" to ¾" diameter straight branches for the rails B, each 20" long.

Laying Out the Sub-Structure

1. Lay all the legs A on the workbench. Using the pencil, make a mark 12" from the bottom of each leg. As an aid to simplify construction, wrap a small piece of masking tape around each leg and mark as follows: A1, A2, A, A3, and A4. Set these aside. NOTE: Before attaching the screw-eyes to the rails, make certain the screw-eyes are able to slip around the legs. If need be, trim a bit of the leg to guarantee the attachment.

2. Place all of the rails B on the workbench. Screw the three- or four-inch metal screw-eye through the ends of all the rails. To help with construction, as above, with masking tape on each part, mark three rails B1; three rails B2; three rails B; and three rails B3. Set these aside.

3. Slip one screw-eye/B1 rail around leg A2 at the 12" mark.

4. Fit the B1 rail against the A1 leg at the 12" mark, and nail together using pilot hole and nail construction.

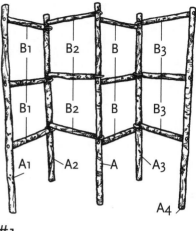

#1

5. Place one screw-eye/B2 rail around leg A at the 12" mark.

6. Fit the B2 rail against the A2 leg at a point just above the rail from step 3; nail to leg A2 with pilot hole and nail construction.

7. Fit the second B1 rail screw-eye part over leg A2 at a point approximately 11" up from the first B1 rail.

8. Using pilot hole and nail construction, attach the B1 rail to the A1 leg at a point 11" up from the first attached B1 rail.

9. Fit the second B2 rail screw-eye part over leg A at a point approximately 11" up from the first B2 rail.

10. Using pilot hole and nail construction, attach the B2 rail to the A2 leg at a point 11" up from the first attached B2 rail.

11. Add the last B1 rail screw-eye part over leg A2 11" up from the previous attached rail.

12. Using pilot hole and nail construction, attach the B1 rail to the A1 leg 11" up from the last attached B1 rail.

13. Add the last B2 rail in the same manner as diagrams 9 and 10 above.

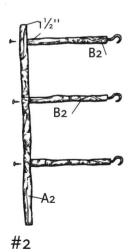

#2

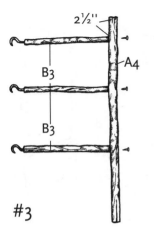

#3

Joining the Parts

1. At the 11" mark on leg A, at a point just below the bottom B2 screw-eye, butt bottom rail B against leg A and nail in place. Butt the same rail B, against leg A3 at the 11" mark; using pilot hole and nail construction, nail rail B to leg A3.
2. Slip screw-eye rail B3 over leg A3 just above installed B rail.
3. Butt bottom B3 rail against Leg A4, and attach with pilot hole and nail construction.
4. Butt rail B against leg A, just below the middle installed rail B2, and attach to leg A and to leg A3 with pilot hole and nail construction.
5. Slip the middle screw-eye B3 rail over leg A3, just above the middle B rail.
6. Using pilot hole and nail construction, attach the B3 rail to leg A4 at a point 11" up from the first B3 rail.
7. Butt the remaining B rail against leg A, just below the top attached B2 rail; using pilot hole and nail construction, attach B to leg A just below the top B2 rail, and to leg A3 at approximately 11" above the center B rail.

Completing the Structure

1. Butt the bottom rail B3 against leg A4 at the 12" mark, and join with pilot hole and nail construction.
2. Repeat step 1 with the center rail B3 at a point 11" up; repeat with the remaining rail B3 at 11".
3. Slip the three extended screw-eye B3 rails over leg A3. They will sit just above the three installed rails B.

NOTE: The sections should be able to move easily to allow for folding.

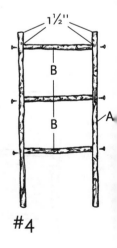

#4

Mini Chair
Plant Stand

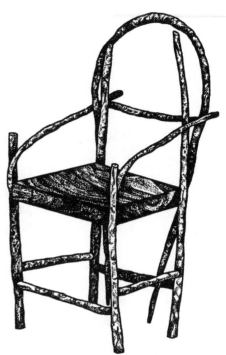

I have a garden of my own,
But so with roses overgrown,
And lilies that you would it guess
To be a little wilderness.

ANDREW MARVEL

THIS PINT-SIZE BENTWOOD CHAIR LENDS RUSTIC CHARM wherever it is placed—on a kitchen shelf, a bedside stand, or a window sill. A piece of scrap lumber, some willow twigs, and birch bark trim combine to create a platform for tiny plants or fresh cut flowers.

MATERIALS   *Skill Level: beginner*
You will need pliable branches such as willow, alder, mulberry, or hickory. Lengths will range from 4" to 31", and branches should be ⅛" to ½" in diameter, including two matched forked branches to form the front legs/arms. Wood scraps 5 ½" × 6 ½", and ¾"

thick are required for the seats, along with pieces of 1" wide birch bark for trim. You will also need an assortment of finishing nails. The seat may be painted, if you so choose. There is a pattern piece provided for the seat.

TOOLS

- Clippers or garden shears
- Tack hammer
- Coping saw
- Ruler or measuring tape
- Marking pencil
- Scissors
- Carpenter's glue (white or yellow)
- Work gloves

CUTTING CHART

Name of Part	Quantity	Diameter (inches)	Length	Description (inches)
Back legs A	2	½	13–14	straight
Front legs/arms B	2	½–legs; ¼-arms	8-legs; 7-arms	pliable/ forked
Front/back braces C	2	¼–½	4 ½-back 5 ½-front	straight
Side braces D	2	¼–½	4 ¼	straight
Ladder back E	1	½	4 ½	straight
Bentwood back F	1	¼	31	pliable

DIRECTIONS

Cutting the Branches

1. Cut two ½" diameter branches for the back legs A, each approximately 14" long. NOTE: The length varies between 13" and 14", allowing for the natural crooks and bends on the twig.
2. Cut two pliable and forked branches for the front legs/arms B; the ½" diameter leg, 8" long; and the ¼" diameter arm, 7" long.
3. Cut two ¼" to ½" diameter front/back braces C, 4 ½" long for the back and 5 ½" long for the front.

4. Cut two ¼" to ½" diameter side braces D, each 4 ½" long.
5. Cut one ½" diameter branch for the ladderback E, 4 ½" long.
6. Cut one ¼" diameter pliable branch for the bentwood back F, 31" long.

Building the Chair

NOTE: To use the pattern make two copies on a photocopy machine (or trace two copies); turn one side over and tape together along the center line. Trace outline onto the 5 ½" × 6 ½" piece of wood.

1. Transfer the pattern onto the 5 ½" × 6 ½" piece of wood, and cut the seat corners to size, using the coping saw. NOTE: If you decide to paint the seat, do it before you begin construction.
2. Position the back legs A in the seat back at the two corner cutouts. The legs extend 7" below the seat corner. Using pilot hole construction, nail the two back legs A to the seat back at both corner cutout locations.
3. Position the front legs/arms B in the seat front at the two corner cutouts. The legs extend 6 ¾" below the seat corners at the front. Using pilot hole construction, nail the two front legs B to the seat front at both corner cutout locations.
4. Carefully bend each extended arm toward the corresponding back leg. The arm extends approximately 1 ½" beyond the back leg, and rests against the outside of the leg. The ladderback E is attached at this junction.

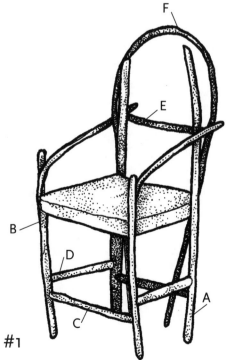

#1

Drill a pilot hole completely through the arm, and the corresponding back leg at the location where they meet, and partway through the ladderback E. Nail all three parts together through the arms.

5. Butt the 4 ½" long back brace between the back legs 2" from the bottom of each leg. Nail in place through the sides of the legs.

6. Butt the 5 ½" long front brace between the front legs 2" from the bottom of each leg. Nail in place through the sides of the legs.

7. Butt the side braces between the front and back legs at 2 ¾" from the bottom of each leg. Nail in place through the front and back of each leg.

8. Center and overlap the bentwood back F against the top of the back legs A, forming a hoop. Carefully bend the ends inside the bottom side braces, and nail the bentwood part F to the seat. Once the bentwood hoop is dry it forms a tight fit against the extended back legs and the outside of the arms. You may, however, decide to nail the hoop to the top of the legs before it dries.

Adding the Trim

Using the scissors, cut 1" wide strips of white birch bark to fit the seat edges. Glue in place and allow to dry overnight.

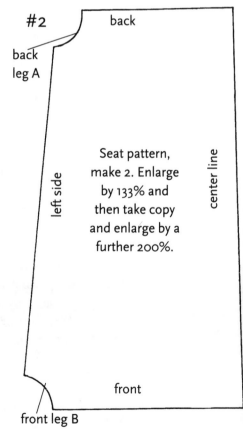

#2   back

back
leg A

left side

Seat pattern, make 2. Enlarge by 133% and then take copy and enlarge by a further 200%.

center line

front

front leg B

Bark Flower Pot Cozy

A nosegay of sweet scented flowers is always an acceptable gift
to visiting friends, especially if they hail from the city.

LOUISE BEEBE WILDER

WRAP YOUR POTS IN NATURAL BEAUTY WITH SCISSORS, GLUE, and sheets of peeled bark. This easy project is perfect for beginners of all ages, and welcomes children to join in the quest for the peeled bark. For gift giving, fill the pots with plants, or tuck in small packets of easy-to-grow seeds or fill with home-made potpourri.

MATERIALS

Skill Level: beginner
You will need peeled birch bark, approximately 5" wide and 15" long for a 4" flowerpot (see pattern) and a dab of glue. Optional materials include raffia or twine for tying the sheet of bark around the flowerpot instead of (or in addition to) the glue.

TOOLS
- Scissors
- Pencil and ruler

DIRECTIONS   NOTE: The following directions are for a four-inch flowerpot. For other size pots, use a photocopy machine to reduce or enlarge the pattern for your pot.

Enlarge the pattern provided by 50%, and trace the outline on the back of the birch bark. Using a pencil, mark the outline of the pattern, and cut to size with the scissors. Arrange and glue the bark in place around the flowerpot. Wrap with raffia, ribbon, or twine if desired.

#1

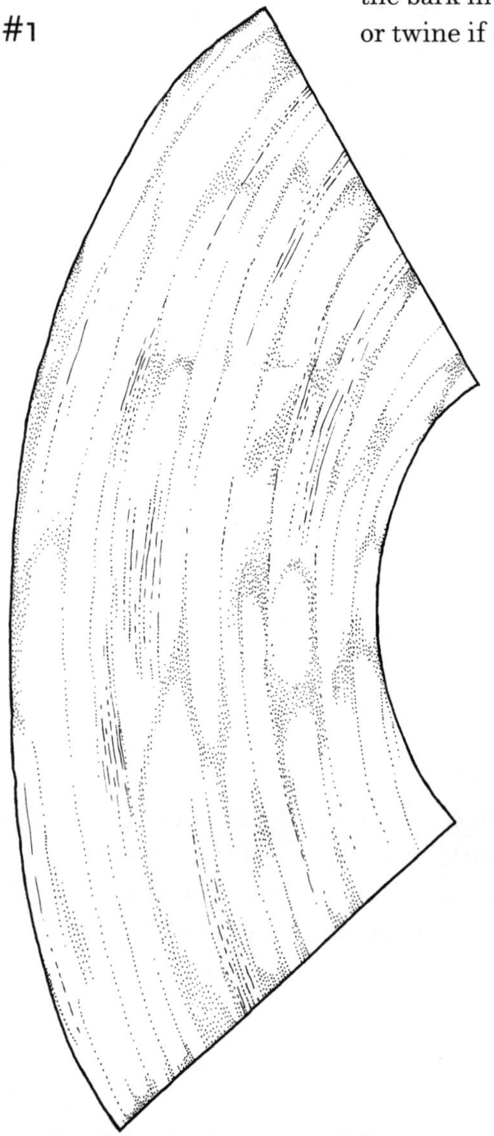

pattern; enlarge
as needed to fit
flowerpot

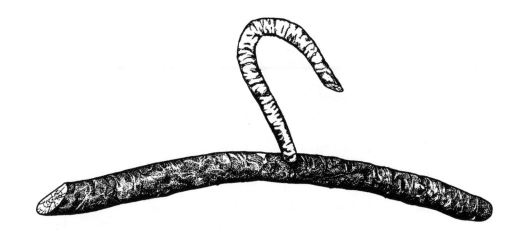

Twig Hanger

PICK UP STICKS AND FASHION THEM INTO USEFUL NATURAL
hangers for hanging up gardening clothes, for drying herbs in
the kitchen, or for dangling lavender sachets near the bath.

MATERIALS

Skill Level: beginner

Try to locate a hardwood branch such as white birch or cherry,
with a slight bend for the arms, approximately 16" long and ¾"
to 1" in diameter. You will also need a pliable twig, such as willow
or alder, approximately 10" long and ½" in diameter for the
hanger hook. You will require ¾" scrap wood and eight common
½" nails for forming the crook in the hanger hook, along with a
dab of white glue to secure the hook in the arm. Pattern pieces
are provided for the hook outline and hanger.

TOOLS
- Crosscut hand saw
- Garden shears or clippers
- Ruler
- Pencil
- Drill with a selection of bits

nails

#1

hanger hook
outline

DIRECTIONS
1. Draw hanger hook outline on the scrap wood. Hammer in the nails so they protrude but stand upright. Arrange the pliable willow hanger hook along the nails. Allow it to dry (approximately 5 to 8 days).
2. Trim all protruding branches, and sand any rough edges on the hardwood branch. Trim and taper the ends, if needed.
3. Enlarge the hanger pattern by 50%. When the hanger hook is completely dry, mark the location for the hook placement on the arm. NOTE: A dry hanger hook is required to ensure a snug fit. Using the drill and correct size bit, drill part way through the hanger arm. Fit the hook in the predrilled arm hole, adjusting the hook end if necessary. When you are satisfied with the fit, add a dab of glue on the hook, and in the hole. If it is loose in the hole, dip the hook in sawdust and then insert it. Allow it to dry overnight.

#2   hanger pattern

Seed

Caddies

SEASONED GARDENERS OFTEN COLLECT AND SAVE SEEDS FROM favorite heirloom plants to sow the following season, or to share with friends. These easy-to-make containers are perfect for storing seeds, or even small trinkets.

MATERIALS

Skill Level: beginner

Choose hardwood branches such as white birch, maple, or cherry, approximately 3" in diameter for the containers, and approximately 1 ½" in diameter for the stoppers. The containers vary in height from 3" to 5", and the stoppers are 1 ½" to 2 ½" long. Tack on brown kraft paper recycled from grocery sacks for the paper labels.

TOOLS
- Crosscut hand saw
- Ruler or measuring tape
- Marking pencil
- Tack hammer and tacks
- Sharp pocket knife for trimming the stoppers
- Sandpaper (optional)
- Vise for holding the branch steady while drilling
- Electric drill with a 1 ⅜" bit, or a hand held carpenter's auger

NOTE: Before the electric drill various tools were employed for boring different-size holes in wood, such as the nose auger, tap auger, or spoon bit. If you have access to an expansive bit, or other suitable hand tool, try using it for this project. Using tools rather than machines may help develop a deeper relationship with your rustic work.

DIRECTIONS

Making the Containers

1. Even out the bottom of the branches so they stand firmly upright. Measure and mark the center top of each branch. NOTE: Precautions should be taken when drilling into the center of a branch. NEVER hold the small branch in your hand while drilling, and if you place a round branch in the jaws of a vise to hold it steady, you will probably crush it or at least mar the bark. A simple woodworking solution is to wrap

stopper

container

#1

the branch with a soft, dense fabric before placing it in the vise. An old towel, or scrap of terry cloth works very well.

2. Using the correct size bit, drill a hole at the center mark of each branch. For a 3" diameter branch, make the opening 2" in diameter, therefore leaving a 1" rim remaining. For a 3" tall branch, drill the opening 1 ½" deep leaving a 1 ½" bottom.

Making the Stoppers

Cut 1 ½" diameter branches 1 ½" to 2 ½" long. Lightly sand the cut edges. Plug the stoppers into the container openings, and use a sharp knife to adjust the fit if necessary. Fill with seeds and tack on labels.

Notes